The World of Stamps and Stamp Collecting

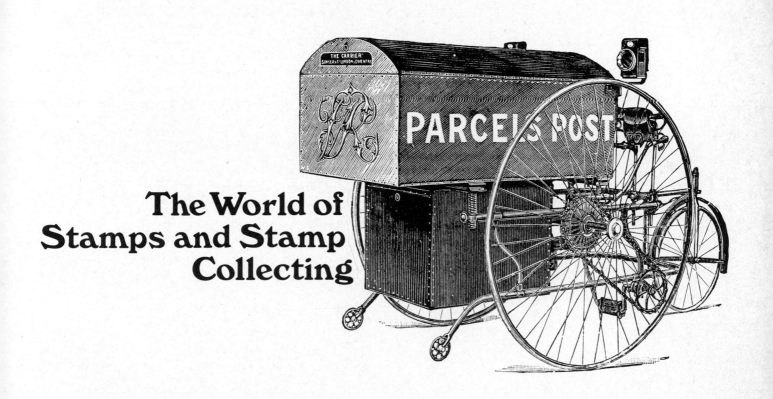

The first coach to carry Royal Mail left the Swan Tavern
in Bristol on August 2, 1784, picked up mail at the Three
Tuns in Bath and arrived at the Swan with Two Necks in
London the following morning. Mail coaches replaced
postboys on horseback. The illustration shows the Bath
mail being carried in early Victorian times

Hamlyn

London · New York · Sydney · Toronto

The World of Stamps and Stamp Collecting

Arthur Blair

Published by
The Hamlyn Publishing Group Limited
London · New York · Sydney · Toronto
Hamlyn House, Feltham, Middlesex, England
© The Hamlyn Publishing Group Limited 1972
ISBN 0 600 379736
Filmset in England by V. Siviter Smith and Co. Ltd.,
Birmingham
Printed in Western Germany
Mohndruck Reinhard Mohn OHG Gütersloh
Mohn Gordon Ltd., London

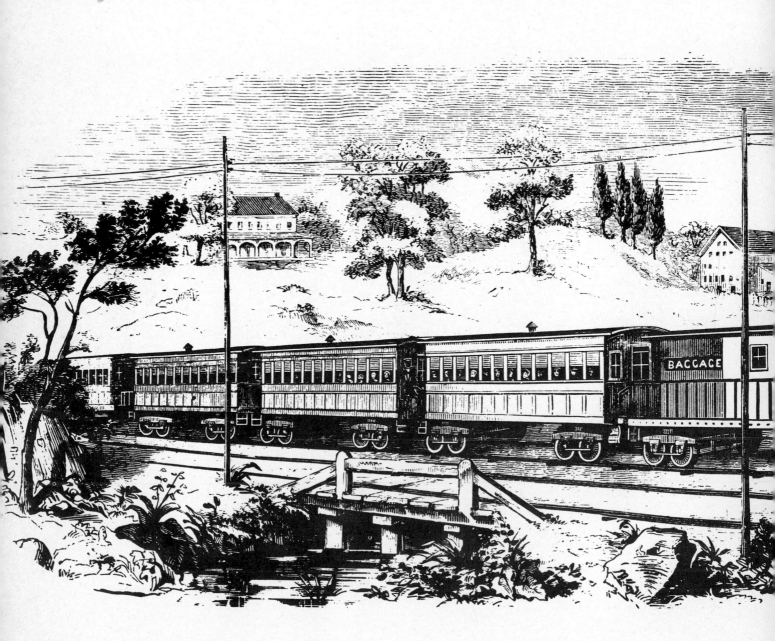

Contents

In the beginning   7

The production of stamps   23

Country and group collecting   39

Thematics and Cinderellas   71

Covers, cards and cancels   87

Collecting postal history 103

Societies, exhibitions, literature 115

Appendix 125

Index 126

Acknowledgments 128

Changing horses outside the Coach Office. On the side
of the mail coach can be seen the route: Glasgow—
Carlisle—Manchester—London. The date is 1843

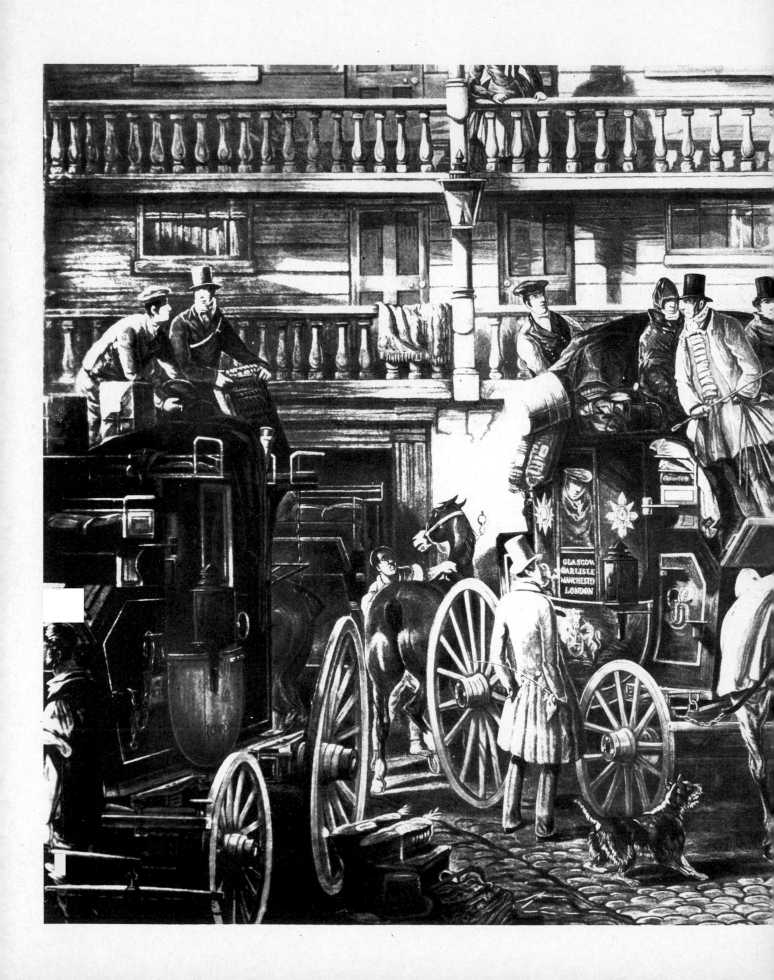

In the beginning

When the postman drops mail through our letter box, we are participating in the benefits of a system of communications that no doubt began in the Stone Age. And it could have been in the following manner. In those far-off days, a virile young female feeling the loneliness of isolated cave life, propelled a chunk of rock in the direction of a lusty young man. The prey having been stunned, the female dragged him by his long hair into her cave to console him with a story that a vicious *stegosaurus ungulatus* (dinosaur) had knocked him silly with a flick of its armoured tail . . . and so began a method of communicating thought to a person some distance away.

Perhaps it was not quite as we have pictured, but that was the basic principle behind primitive message systems: someone wished to convey an idea in the mind to someone else at a distance, a missive was despatched and the recipient got the message, and from that point of contact interesting developments would take place.

Early man soon realised the social and political advantages of communicating with other inhabitants in his sparsely populated wilderness, and how to convert grunts into visual form. There were friends to be summoned to a gathering of the tribe; enemies to be warned that unless they stopped raiding territory that did not belong to them, carrying off their women, cattle and fowls of the air—poultry at that time were good flyers—they would have their hairy heads battered into their sloping shoulders by the thigh bone of a mammoth.

Messages daubed in woad on stone or pieces of bark were probably the first 'letters', followed by more intelligent hieroglyphics scratched on a roughly hewn piece of slate . . . imagination can conjure up various interesting methods by which our primitive ancestors contacted each other over distances in the peaceful days of long, long ago.

Efficiently organised postal services in some form have been known for almost six thousand years, although for much of that time they existed chiefly for rulers and their courts.

About four thousand years before the dawn of Christianity the Babylonians and Assyrians had a court messenger service. Messages were written on clay tablets and other materials, using curious wedge-shape characters known as cuneiform script.

There are references in the Old Testament to the couriers of the king carrying letters and despatches and these give the earliest account of any kind of postal service.

'So the posts went with the letters from the king and his princes throughout all Israel and Judah . . .'
2 Chronicles XXX, 6.

1 Clay tablet found in excavation illustrates the life of Babylon. This 'mosaic standard' is from biblical 'Ur of the Chaldees'

2 In the great days of Greece, letters were carried by couriers, sometimes on foot, sometimes on horseback

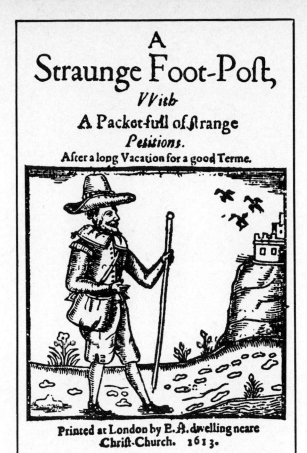

A
Straunge Foot-Poſt,
VVith
A Packet-full of ſtrange
Petitions.
After a long Vacation for a good Terme.

Printed at London by E. A. dwelling neare
Chriſt-Church. 1613.

'for he (King Ahasuerus) sent letters into all the
king's provinces, into every province according
to the writing thereof, and to every people after
their language . . .'
Esther I, 22.

'And the letters were sent by posts into all the
king's provinces . . .'
Esther III, 13.

'The posts went out, being hastened by the
king's commandment . . .'
Esther III, 15.

'And he wrote in the king Ahasuerus' name,
and sealed it with the king's ring, and sent
letters by posts on horseback, and riders on
mules, camels, and young dromedaries.'
Esther VIII, 10.

'So the posts that rode upon mules and camels
went out, being hastened and pressed on by
the king's commandment.'
Esther VIII, 14. (This passage is a little difficult
to appreciate, for the king's posts are supposed
to have gone at a great speed for long
distances, but the pace of a camel is said to be
about three miles an hour, and a mule dislikes
being rushed!)

The Egyptians wrote on clay tablets and to
them is given the credit of having invented a
type of writing paper from the split reeds of the
papyrus plant. Vast quantities of papyrus letters
stored at Tell-el-Amarna came to light during
archaelogical discoveries in the 19th century.
In the 5th century BC, the Medes and Persians
had a highly organised relay postal service of
men and horses stationed at a distance of a
day's journey between posts (positus—placed
at fixed intervals) along the main routes from
Persepolis. The Greeks borrowed the horse-
relay system from the Persians, but preferred
foot-runners to carry important letters from one
city state to another. Alexander the Great
adapted the best features of the Greek foot-
post and the Persian horse-post in order to
maintain efficient communications throughout
his vast empire. The men on foot were tough
and reliable, those on a steed were famed for
their speed and regularity in the safe delivery of
letters entrusted to them.

For their lines of communication the Romans
at first used messengers on foot, but as their
Empire grew in size, and the administration
became more complex, the volume of correspondence between the Emperor and the
provincial governors required a more efficient
system. As a result cursores, or foot-postmen,
were employed on local routes, while veredarii,
or horse-postmen, were used on longer routes.
The Romans had the advantage of an excellent

road system, which permitted the development of postal wagons, anticipating the mail-coaches of the 18th century.

In the Far East the Chinese operated a court postal system at least a thousand years before Christ. The earliest letters were carved on bamboo staves and examples of these primitive letters have been discovered in archaeological excavations.

After the fall of the Roman Empire several centuries were to pass before a postal service re-appeared in Western Europe. Charlemagne established a postal service in his empire in the early 9th century. Subsequently the Church established a postal service to link abbeys and monasteries with Rome. At that time few people other than the clergy were able to read or write. In the 12th century the first of the great European universities, at Padua, Bologna and Paris, organised their own postal services. Merchant communities in the Hanseatic ports of Hamburg and Bremen, and the Venetian Republic operated postal systems for business reasons.

By the 15th century the king and his court, the Church, the universities and the merchants all had postal services for their own benefit, but the general public was normally excluded. However as the people became more literate a service for the use of everyone became essential. The earliest public services appeared about 1450 in the Italian principalities and various parts of the Holy Roman Empire. Gradually the family of the Counts of Thurn and Taxis developed a network of posts in the Empire, stretching from the Black Sea to the English Channel, and from Italy to the Baltic. Even after the Empire distintegrated the Thurn and Taxis administration continued to operate its services all over Western Europe, until 1867 when the last remnants of the system were purchased by the Prussian government.

The earliest purely national service was established by Louis XI in 1464, but just over a hundred years elapsed before the general public was allowed to participate.

King Henry IV established a regular postal system in England at the beginning of the 15th century, but it existed solely for the use of the government. It was not until 1516 that a public service was introduced, for in that year Sir Brian Tuke was appointed Master of the Posts. At first the only regular route lay from London to Dover, but gradually postal services were extended along the major roads of the country, from London to Plymouth, Chester and York. From 1581 onwards letters from private individuals were permitted to be carried in the official mailbags. The mail was carried by post-boys mounted on horses.

In the reign of King James I (1603–25) letters from London to Edinburgh cost 8d each and

4

5

6

4 A method of carrying mail in France in the 15th century was by boat. The river system often provided more convenient routes than the road system
5,6 These two Indian stamps are from a series of eight issued in 1937 which were the first to show King George VI. The series illustrated mail transport in India from earliest times, the two examples being of a Dak runner and a Dak tonga

London 1661

 Dublin 1672

 Edinburgh 1693

 Exeter 1698

 Bristol 1705

 New York 1758

 Philadelphia 1767

 Boston 1769

 Charlestown 1774

 Albany 1774

 Quebec 1776

 Calcutta 1776

7 The London International Stamp Exhibition of 1960 commemorated the tercentenary of the appointment of Colonel Henry Bishop, first Postmaster-General of the United Kingdom, 1660–1663, with 12 souvenir 'stamps' bearing Bishop marks, the first post office stamps at the places indicated
8 Colonel Henry Bishop introduced the Bishop mark in 1661
9 Part of a pamphlet by William Dockwra announcing his famous Penny Post service in the City of London in 1680

7

8

9

A PENNY
Well Beſtowed,

Or a Brief Account of the *New Deſign* contrived for the great Increaſe of *Trade*, and Eaſe of *Correſpondence*, to the great Advantage of the Inhabitants of all ſorts, by Conveying of *LETTERS* or *PACQVETS* under a Pound Weight, to and from all parts within the Cities of *London* and *Weſtminſter*; and the Out Pariſhes within the VVeekly Bills of *Mortality*,

For One Penny.

 Here is nothing tends more to the increaſe of Trade and Buſineſs than a Speedy, Cheap, and ſafe way of *Intelligence*, much being obſtructed and more retarded in all Places where that is wanting. For as Money, like the Blood in Natural Bodies, gives Life to Trade by its Circulation; ſo Correſpondence like the Vital Spirits, gives it Senſe and Motion: and the more that theſe abound in any Place, the more doth that Place increaſe in Riches, Strength, and Vigor.

But in this Age it is not to be expected that any New Deſign can be contrived for the Publick Good, without meeting many raſh Cenſures and Impediments, from the Fooliſh and Malicious; therefore 'twas not likely this ſhould eſcape that common Fate. Yet We hope to all the reaſonable and Candid, who are willing to underſtand their own Intereſt, this Paper may be Satisfactory.

For 'tis undertaken by the Methods of that Correſpondency ſettled, that any Perſon may promiſe himſelf his *Letter* or *Pacquet* ſhall ſafely come to any place directed to, lying within the Cities and Suburbs of *London* and *VVeſtminſter*, and all their contiguous Buildings; alſo to *VVapping*, *Ratcliffe*, *Lyme-houſe*, *Poplar* and *Blackwall*; to *Redriffe*, *Southwark*, and ſo to *Newington* and *Lambeth*; to *Hackney*, *Iſlington*; and all other places within the *Weekly Bills* of *Mortality*, be it farther or nearer, to and from any of the aforeſaid Places,

For One Penny.

The times for iſſuing out of *Letters* to any of the aforeſaid Places, to be in the Summer time from Six in the Morning to Nine at Night, and at reaſonable hours agreeable to the Winter Seaſon.

To the moſt remote Places *Letters* ſhall be ſent at leaſt Five times a day.

To Places of quick Negotiation within the City, and in the Term time for ſervice of the Law Buſineſs, &c. at leaſt Fifteen times a day.

No *Letters* that come after Nine at Night, to be delivered till next Morning (except ſuch Letters as are for the *Poſt-Office General*.)

By this means all Perſons, as well Gentlemen, Lawyers, Shop-keepers, and Handi-crafts Men, that make and deal in Commodities vended by Patterns and poor Priſoners, and all others, have that diſpatched for a *Penny*, which uſually coſts Three Pence, Six Pence, or a Shilling. Now to oblige Men to pay more when they can hereby be cheaper ſerved, were to im-poſe an illegal Tax upon the Inhabitants without their Conſents.

Beſides many Journeys of Taylors, Weavers, and other poor Artificers, and their Servants, will be ſpared, who now conſume much time abroad in going to and fro, to the im-poveriſhing of their Families, becauſe they cannot extravagantly pay a Porter for a Meſſage,

11

took up to four days on the weekly journey. During this reign there were two Postmasters: Lord Stanhope controlled the inland posts, while Matthew de Quester handled the foreign mail. De Quester's successor, Thomas Witherings, became Chief Postmaster in 1632 and during his tenure in office he tried to establish the carriage of mail as a government monopoly. Until that time anyone who chose to could carry letters, but this was expressly forbidden by an Act of 1657, which established the General Post Office. This act was confirmed after the Restoration of King Charles II in 1660 and the General Letter Office (afterwards known as the General Post Office) was established.

Colonel Henry Bishop was appointed Postmaster General in January 1661 on a seven years' lease, and it was he who originated the postmark. Complaints had been received of letters being delayed in the post, and in order to overcome this problem Colonel Bishop invented a small circular mark containing the day and month of the date. The Bishop mark was first used in London and subsequently adopted by Dublin, Edinburgh and a number of cities in America and India. It was simple but effective and remained in use for well over a century.

By the end of the 17th century postmarks showing the name of the post office were coming into use. The earliest types consisted of curved or straight-line marks merely giving the name. Later marks also incorporated the distance from London, since distance was one of the factors governing the amount of postage charged on a letter. These mileage marks gradually died out at the beginning of the 19th century, though they remained in use somewhat later in Scotland.

Other countries were relatively slow in adopting postmarks. The Dutch East Indies Company used a postmark showing its VOC monogram from 1667 onwards, but France did not adopt postmarks until 1695 and other countries were even later.

As a rule the postage on a letter was paid by the recipient, not the sender. The amount of postage was estimated according to the weight of the letter or the number of sheets (the wrapper or envelope being counted as an additional sheet) and according to the distance carried. Other charges might include a penny for local delivery and an additional halfpenny charged on any letters in Scotland conveyed in a vehicle with more than two wheels.

Postal charges rose rapidly in Britain during the early years of the 19th century. A letter carried a short distance was charged 4d—then equal to a labourer's daily wage—while a letter from Edinburgh to London might cost several shillings (the equivalent of several pounds

10 The *cavallini*, 'little horseman' stamps of Sardinia, values 15, 25 and 50c. Used from 1818, the 'stamps' were methods of taxing correspondence, and did not represent postal charges

11 Three Dockwra marks of the 1680s. The first means 'eight in the morning' and the second 'four in the afternoon'. The 'L' in the third means the chief office, Lyme Street

12 Three 'Free' Franks, the first of Dublin, 26 October 1810; the second is of 14 April 1791; the third of 11 November 1829

13 A British post office in 1790, from 'The Jubilee of Penny Postage' (1890)
14 An additional charge of ½d was made in 1813 on mail coach letters in Scotland
15 The General Post Office, St. Martin's-le-Grand at the beginning of the 19th century

14

15

16 Country letter carrier from a painting of 1842. The Post Office had its origin in royal couriers who carried the King's despatches, therefore England's royal colour, red, was chosen for the uniforms

17 English mail coach guard. The service began in 1784 and this print is dated 1832. Guards were issued with pistols, a blunderbuss, a cutlass, a post-horn and a time-piece. The last coach ran in 1845

15

today) if it consisted of more than one sheet. Members of Parliament, however, enjoyed a franking privilege. This meant that they could send letters free through the post, merely by adding their signature to the bottom left-hand corner of the letter. MPs would often give signed sheets of paper to friends or their constituents in order to win votes at elections. The abuse of this system is explained in the chapter on Collecting Postal History.

The high postal rates also encouraged people to evade postage by having their letters carried privately. Thousands of pounds were lost to the country's revenue each year by this infringement of the Postmaster General's monopoly. This problem was common to many countries in the early 19th century, though it was probably most acute in Britain where a high level of literacy, combined with the rapid development of commerce after the Industrial Revolution, made postal reform essential.

Various schemes for reforming the system were proposed from the 1820s onwards. Robert Wallace, MP for Greenock; James Chalmers, a Dundee publisher and bookseller, and Rowland Hill, a Kidderminster schoolmaster, were among those who put forward proposals for reform. The movement gathered momentum from 1834 onwards. Rowland Hill's recommendations seemed revolutionary—nothing less than a Uniform Penny Post. At that time local penny posts operated in and around many towns, while the London area, being much larger, had a twopenny post. Within these areas letters were carried at the much reduced rate of one penny and were often prepaid in cash. The special postmarks of the penny posts are of great interest to philatelists.

Rowland Hill advocated a flat rate of one penny for a one ounce letter, regardless of the distance it travelled. By greatly simplifying the postal charges he paved the way for the prepayment of postage by means of special envelopes or wrappers and by means of adhesive labels which could be stuck on the letter and handed in at any post office. A great deal of controversy has raged over the vexed question of who first thought of adhesive stamps. One school of thought gives credit to Chalmers, though it now seems that he devised stamps independent of, but later than, Hill.

On the continent of Europe several people also thought of the idea about the same time. As long ago as 1653 Renouard de Velayer operated a Petit Post in Paris and used small wafers sold for two sous (about a penny) to indicate that the postage was prepaid. No examples of the so-called *Billets Port Paye* used by this post have yet to come to light, though they undoubtedly existed. Should anyone eventually discover one of these *Billets Port Paye*, it would create a sensation in the world of stamps and stamp collecting!

Postal stationery was used in Sardinia from 1818 onwards. Letter sheets were stamped with a device showing a horseman and were sold for 15, 25 or 50 centesimi, according to the distance the missive was to be carried. These 'stamps' represented a government tax on correspondence and had nothing to do with the postage itself, so the *Cavallini* ('little horsemen') cannot be regarded as postage stamps in the true sense. Stamped postal stationery made its debut in Sydney, New South Wales, in 1838; it consisted of letter sheets bearing the embossed coat of arms of the colony. This idea was borrowed by the governor of the colony from the proposals of Rowland Hill, but it was not very popular. Used examples of these sheets are rare.

Rowland Hill's proposals were accepted by the British government in 1839 and the Treasury held a competition for the design of the proposed stamps. Over 2,000 entries were sent in, but in the end it was the simple rectangle bearing a profile of Queen Victoria, suggested by Hill himself, which was adopted. As a transitional measure a Uniform Fourpenny rate was introduced in December 1839, and reduced to a Uniform Penny rate in January 1840. The adhesive stamps and special pictorial wrappers were not ready by that time, so hand-struck markings continued in use for a further four months. The Penny Black and Twopenny Blue went on sale on 1 May 1840 and were valid for postage from 6 May onwards. The prepayment of postage remained optional for several years, to give people a chance to get used to the idea, but unpaid letters were charged double postage to the recipient, a custom that has been retained for unpaid or underpaid letters to this day.

Adhesive stamps were an immediate success, though several years passed before the Uniform Penny Postage scheme began to make a profit for the Post Office. The pictorial envelopes and wrappers, designed by William Mulready, were ridiculed by press and public and frequently parodied by caricaturists, and so they were withdrawn from use in 1841, being replaced by envelopes bearing an embossed stamp.

Other countries watched the developments in Great Britain very closely, though some time elapsed before the idea was adopted elsewhere. The first adhesive stamps to appear outside Britain were produced in the United States in 1842, for an official local delivery service (Carriers) known as the New York City Despatch Post, and it was not until 1847 that the United States Post Office introduced stamps for use throughout the country. In the intervening years stamps were issued by many private letter carriers and despatch companies and, from 1845 onwards, by several of the

18 General Post Office uniforms of the early Victorian era
19 Sir Rowland Hill, generally acknowledged to be the man who perfected the idea of an adhesive postage stamp
20 Sorting letters by hand at the Inland Office of the GPO in early Victorian days

18

19

20

21 3 grote value of Bremen issued April 10, 1855
22 1856–63 Bremen 5 grote used on foreign mail routed through Great Britain
23 Bremen bright green of October 20, 1859, value 5 sgr used on foreign mail
24 1866–67 Bremen 10 grote, one of the last Bremen stamps before it joined the North German Confederation

25 A design by Chalmers for a stamp for the Treasury competition in 1839, with the type of cancellation he suggested
26 The steamship *Lady McLeod* carried post privately between Port of Spain and San Fernando from 1847–49 and issued this stamp, now much sought after

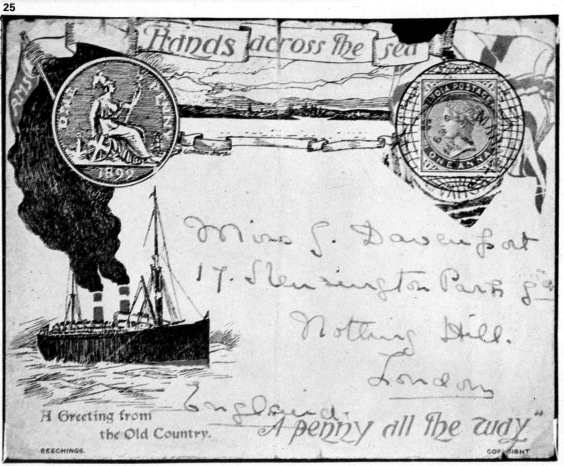

27 An envelope to commemorate the adoption of the Imperial Penny Postage was published by Beeching in England in 1899. This cover was sent from Mahableshwar to London on May 1, 1899
28 The Bellman was an early substitute for the street pillar box. He would patrol the streets ringing his bell and people would bring him their letters. Bellmen were originally 'pirate' rivals to the Post Office, but were suppressed, and then the idea was taken over by the Post Office itself

United States postmasters, including those of New York, St Louis and Baltimore.

The first postal administration to follow Britain's lead was in the Western Hemisphere when, in 1843, Brazil issued the famous 'Bulls-eyes' in denominations of 30, 60 and 90 reis. Like the British stamps the name of the country did not appear in the design. In the early years postage stamps were valid only in the country which issued them, so there was no need to add the name to the design. After the foundation of the Universal Postal Union in 1874 it was decreed that the country name had to appear on the stamps. As a mark of honour to Britain for inventing stamps, she alone was permitted to issue stamps without a name on them and to this day the portrait of the reigning monarch is held to be sufficient identification. In 1843 two Swiss cantons began issuing stamps. Zurich issued 4 and 6 rappen stamps in a plain numeral design, while Geneva produced a curious double stamp, each half of which featured the cantonal coat of arms and was worth 5 centimes. As an incentive to the customer the complete stamp, known to collectors as the Double Geneva, was sold at the reduced rate of 8 centimes. The Swiss canton of Basle followed in 1845, with a handsome stamp featuring the cantonal arms and known for this reason as the Basle Dove.

In 1847 two British colonies began issuing stamps. In April of that year a blue label, with a nominal value of 5 cents, was issued for use on letters carried between Port of Spain and San Fernando in Trinidad. The stamp bore a picture of the steamship *Lady McLeod*. This was a private issue and it was not until 1851 that the Trinidad postal administration adopted stamps. In September 1847 Mauritius introduced 1d and 2d stamps, modelled roughly on the contemporary British stamps, but engraved locally by a half-blind watchmaker named James Barnard. Very few of these primitive stamps were produced and the so-called Post Office Mauritius stamps now rank among the world's rarest specimens.

The following year the postmasters of St Georges and Hamilton, in the island of Bermuda, produced their own stamps, though it was not until 1865 that stamps were generally adopted for use in that colony.

Three European countries began issuing stamps in 1849—France with the 'Ceres' design, Belgium with the famous 'Epaulettes' portrait of King Leopold, and Bavaria with the black One Kreuzer. Stamped stationery was introduced in Finland, Russia and Thurn and Taxis administration in the 1840s, though some years elapsed before they adopted adhesive stamps. Stamps spread to the Australian colonies of Victoria and New South Wales in 1850. Two years later Asia's first stamps, the 'Scinde

29 The famous Great Britain Penny Black of 1840, the world's first postage stamp

Scotland   Channel Isles   Leeds

Manchester   Mullingar   Wotton Under Edge

Norwich and Plymouth   York   Kilmarnock

Dublin   Belfast   Cork

30 With the issue of the Penny Black came the necessity for an official cancellation. The Maltese Cross cancellation, believed to be adapted from the Tudor Rose, came into being. Many types existed: there were local variations and different colours, commonest being black and red. Those here were printed on a card by the Great Britain Philatelic Society for the London International Stamp Exhibition, 1960

31

31—39 A selection of early rare stamps:
31 Block of four Hanover 10 gr King George V stamps of 1861
32 Spanish stamp of 1850 showing Queen Isabella II
33 Canadian 6d Prince Albert stamp of 1851
34 Swiss 15 rappen stamp of 1854
35 Nova Scotia 1851 stamp showing Queen Victoria
36 New Brunswick stamp of 1851 showing the Royal Crown and heraldic flowers of the UK
37 Tuscany 1 crazia stamp of 1851
38 3k Wurtemberg stamp of 1851
39 Prussia 1 sgr stamp of 1850—56 showing King Frederick William IV

Dawks', appeared in what is now West Pakistan. They were circular in shape and embossed with the trade mark of the East India Company and issued under the authority of the Commissioner of Scinde, Sir Bartle Frere. They had local validity only and were suppressed in 1854, when stamps were introduced throughout British India.

The first stamps of the African continent appeared in 1853, when the Cape of Good Hope Triangulars were released.

By the end of the 1850s postage stamps had spread into every corner of the globe, though their use was by no means general. No fewer than 70 different countries and postal administrations adopted stamps in that decade, joined by another 60 countries and administrations in the 1860s. By the end of the classic period (1870) only the more remote and backward countries had not introduced stamps, and by that time stamp collecting had progressed beyond a mere 'scrap-book' novelty of schoolboys and young ladies of leisure to become a serious pursuit of men in all walks of life.

In the 1860s the first catalogues and magazines became established and the first philatelic societies had been founded. Stamp dealers were in operation as early as the mid-1850s. Stanley Gibbons, now one of the largest philatelic companies in the world, was founded in 1856 when young Edward Stanley Gibbons began dealing in stamps as a sideline to his father's pharmacy in Plymouth. J. B. Moens in Paris, Arthur Maury in Brussels and J. W. Scott in New York also became established about the same time.

Since 1840 there have been over 500 postal administrations. With political changes and amalgamations countries have come and gone and many are remembered today only by the stamps they left behind them. At the present time there are some 230 different postal administrations issuing over 6,000 stamps annually. The humble postage stamp, once intended merely to indicate the prepayment of postage, is now used to raise money for impoverished governments, to finance charitable works, to commemorate famous people, to illustrate a way of life or to preach a political message.

And the number of collectors of these coloured bits of paper runs into many, many millions.

32

33

34

35

36

37

38

39

The north country mails at the Peacock, Islington, in 1823. From a coloured aquatint after a painting by James Pollard. Engraved by T. Sutherland

A stamp may look simple and straightforward, but the newcomer to the hobby will soon discover that there are several factors which can vary. Two stamps, seemingly identical, may in fact differ in several respects: the paper, watermark, perforation and the method of printing may differ. Any one of these differences can affect the value of the stamp, so it is important to be able to detect them. The simplified stamp catalogues, such as Stanley Gibbons' *Stamps of the World*, do not differentiate between the various printings of a stamp or series, but the more advanced catalogues usually list stamps separately, according to differences in their composition or method of printing. Specialised catalogues, of course, go into the subject in depth.

Postage stamps (with a few notable exceptions discussed later) are printed on paper of some kind. To the uninitiated, paper is just paper, but close observation will reveal the subtle characteristics of different types of paper which are important to the stamp collector. First of all the thickness of the paper may vary, from the very thin, hard paper known to philatelists as 'pelure' (French for 'skin') to the very thick, stiff paper known as cartridge or carton. In between there are variations of thickness, softness and porosity, all of which may be significant. The paper may be hand-made and vary in thickness from one end of the sheet to the other.

The stamps of the Indian States and many Oriental countries are usually described as being on 'native' paper—a term which indicates paper ranging in quality from a fine rice paper to a thick, crude, uneven texture.

Machine-made paper may be consistent in its appearance but either laid or wove, depending on the pattern of the fibres. In laid paper the fibres lie in parallel lines, whereas in wove paper the fibres have a knitted texture, like a piece of cloth. These differences are produced by the fine wires or gauze on which the paper pulp is spread during the manufacturing process. Where the lines are grouped at regular intervals, divided by a wider space, the paper is said to be bâtonné (French for 'ruled'), since the regular appearance of the wider line enabled people to write in straight lines.

The quality of paper used in printing stamps may vary from the expensive rag paper, on which many of the classic stamps were produced, to the modern paper made from wood-pulp or esparto grass with a high kaolin content to give it that smooth, glossy texture necessary for the multicolour printing processes now in use.

The content of the paper may depend on security requirements. Many stamps produced for Britain and her colonies by De La Rue were printed on chalk-surfaced paper, to defeat

40 The Great Britain 1840 One Penny rouletted 12 by Henry Archer

41 The most famous stamp printing press in the world, the Perkins Bacon machine on which the Penny Black was printed. It is at present in the British Museum

42 The first perforated stamp of Great Britain, the One Penny red-brown of 1850 perforated by Henry Archer. A cover from the Royal Collection

24

43

44

43–48 Colloidal graphite printing:

43 A printing unit. The lined paper is being printed. The ink pump is in the foreground.

44 The re-wind end of the machine shows the lined stamp paper being re-reeled in preparation for gumming

45 An Avometer checks the electrical conductivity of the graphite

46 Printed on a continuous web, the stamps are illuminated at the back so that the graphite lines show up in relation to the stamp design

47 A general view of a letter facing machine

48 Stamp with two lines of colloidal graphite printed vertically at the back

45

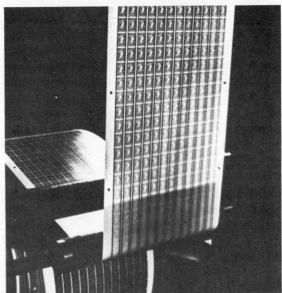

46

47

attempts by dishonest persons to remove the postmark and re-use the stamps. Many of these stamps may be found on ordinary or chalk-surfaced paper, thus it is important to be able to detect the latter—not only because it may affect the value of the stamp, but because great care must be taken in soaking off paper from used stamps. Chalk-surfaced paper may be detected by means of a silver pencil, though the edge of a pure silver coin will do just as well. Obviously care should be exercised when testing a paper in this manner, for silver leaves a faint black mark on chalk-surfaced paper.

Nowadays paper treated with a luminescent substance is used in many countries in connection with the automatic sorting of mail. Special 'Helecon' paper is used in Australia for stamps, while other countries, such as Germany, Denmark, Switzerland and the United States, use luminescent or fluorescent paper. As a rule these stamps circulate only in those areas where electronic sorting of mail takes place. So, once more, there may be two distinct varieties of a stamp, though they appear identical without the aid of a quartz lamp.

British stamps used in electronic experiments were released in 1957 with vertical black lines on the back. These lines, known as Naphthadag (the last three letters being the initials of Defloculated Acheson's Graphite) were easy to detect. They were superseded in the 1960s by phosphor bands printed on the face of the stamp, which can be detected by holding the stamp at an angle to the light. A similar system is used in Canada, where specimens so treated are said to be 'tagged'.

There are also many different kinds of paper. Collectors of New Zealand stamps, for example, have to learn how to distinguish between Cowan, Jones and Wiggins-Teape papers, all of which were used to produce certain stamps at various times. For reference purposes it is a useful idea to make a type collection of different papers: sugar-bag paper (British Guiana), newsprint (wartime Jersey), gold-beaters' skin (Germany), transparent paper (Saxony, 1946), *bleuté* or blued paper (the early stamps of Britain), or granite paper—in which there are tiny hairs—(Switzerland, Austria). The first stamps of Latvia were printed on the back of German war maps or unfinished Bolshevik banknotes.

In 1958 Hungary issued a miniature sheet in honour of the Brussels Fair and printed the stamps on wax-cloth. In 1955 the same country released a 5 forint stamp printed on silver paper, appropriately marking the Light Metal Industries International Congress. Silver paper has also been used on stamps issued by Russia and Sharjah. Metal foil (usually gold or silver) has been used for coin-shaped stamps released by Tonga, Bhutan, Sharjah, Sierra Leone and various other countries in the last ten years. Metal foil stamps in more orthodox rectangular shapes have also appeared in a number of states in the French Community, usually in honour of such men as Albert Schweitzer or General De Gaulle.

Bhutan has experimented with several other gimmicks in recent years. These have included stamps printed on thin sheet steel (in honour of the steel industry), on silk, on plastics simulating the texture of oil paintings or creating the three-dimensional effect of sculpture, or in laminated plastics to create an illusion of space.

Watermarks

The special security paper used in stamp production has often incorporated a watermark, a device which is usually visible when the stamp is held up to the light. A watermark is made from a piece of metal or wire (known as the bit) which is attached to the dandy roll under which the paper pulp is squeezed during the manufacturing process. This makes the paper slightly thinner at that particular point, so that when a sheet of paper is held up to the light the thinner areas show up in the form of watermarks.

The watermarks encountered on stamps may be of several types. First of all there is that of the paper-maker; this may consist of the name of the company or its trade-mark. Usually this watermark only appears once on the entire sheet and thus only a letter, or a portion of a letter, may appear on any one stamp.

The second type of watermark is a simple one, in which a single device appears on each stamp, as distinct from the third type which is known as a multiple watermark, showing up as an over-all pattern of devices.

The early British stamps had a watermark of a crown. From 1912 till 1958 the watermark showed the royal monogram as well, but from 1958 till 1967 the monogram was omitted. Since then British stamps have been printed on unwatermarked paper. The so-called Wilding definitive stamps of Britain, in use between 1952 and 1967, were produced with three different watermarks at various times: Tudor crown and monogram, St Edward's crown and monogram, St Edward's crown without monogram. Since the rarity or otherwise of these stamps depends largely on the watermark, it is important to be able to tell them apart.

The earliest colonial stamps had a star watermark, but gradually a crown and the initials CC (Crown Colonies) or CA (Crown Agents) was adopted. As the colonies acquired their independence they substituted their own national emblems, such as the pineapple (Jamaica) or the cockerel (Malawi) or letters like FN (Federation of Nigeria) or PTM (Persekutuan Tanah Melayu—Federation of

49 British Penny Red with experimental separation invented by Henry Archer

50

51

53

52

50 Part of a sheet of the 6c Netherlands definitive series of 1926—31 showing interrupted perforation. At each corner of each stamp holes are missing on the lateral perforation
51 Bhutan stamp in honour of the steel industry printed on thin sheet steel
52 Bhutan stamp from a paintings series in which the stamps show the full relief effect of an oil painting
53 Bhutan stamp on laminated prismatic-ribbed plastic showing tropical fishes

54

55

54,55 Both sides of a 1920 Latvian stamp which was printed on the back of unfinished banknotes
56,57 Both sides of a block of four Latvian 5k stamps of 1918, which were printed on abandoned German military maps

56

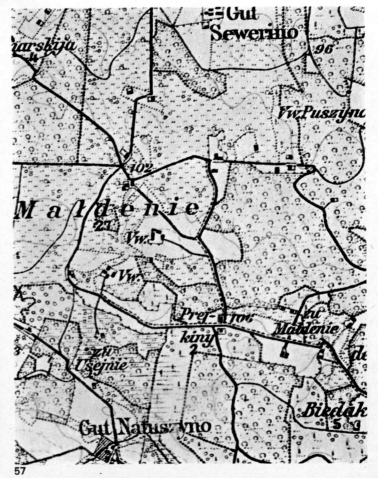

57

58–62 The creation of a United Nations stamp:
58 The engraver uses a pantograph to reduce the drawing to the size of the postage stamp

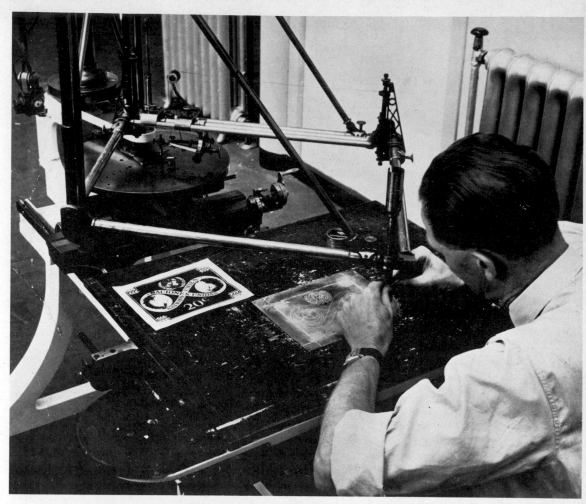

59 Using a strong magnifying glass, the engraver carefully prepares the steel plate. It is said that there are only about a hundred highly skilled stamp and banknote engravers in the world

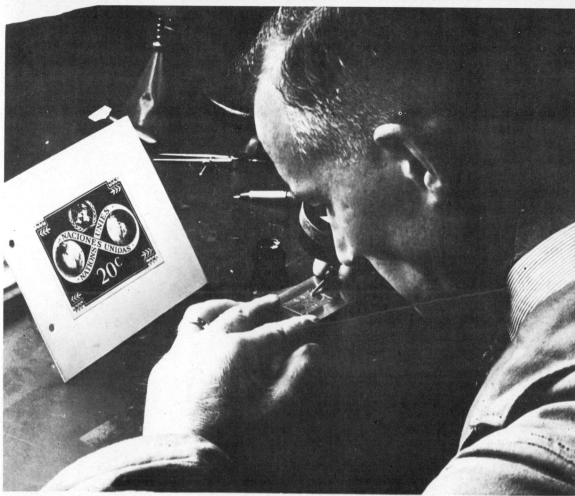

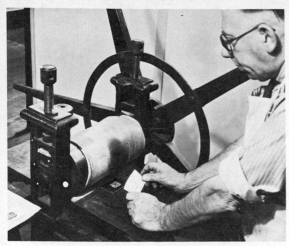

60 A test proof is made by hand from the original die. If satisfactory the plate is hardened and an impression of it transferred to a soft steel roller

61 The roller die rolls in a hundred impressions onto the printing plate, which will be used in the actual printing of the stamp

62 The printed sheet in two panes of 50 impressions comes off the press

Malaya). France has never used a watermark, and the United States had watermarks for a brief period only.

The necessity for this security precaution is not so great nowadays, when modern printing techniques are sufficiently fool-proof to defeat the would-be forger.

As a rule the watermark can be easily detected by holding the stamp up to the light, or by laying it face downwards on a plain, dark surface. If this fails, a watermark detector may be used. In its simplest form this is a small tray of black lacquered metal or plastic, or a tile. The stamp is placed face down in the tray and a drop of benzine put on the back. This renders the stamp temporarily transparent and the watermark should show up clearly. Unfortunately this method cannot be used on stamps printed by photogravure, since benzine acts as a thinner on printing ink and would rapidly dissolve the design.

There are several electric watermark detectors on the market. By means of a light and various coloured filters a faint watermark usually can be detected.

In most stamps the watermark appears in the upright position, but certain coil or booklet stamps have a sideways watermark, and inverted watermarks are quite normal in stamps from booklets. In some cases, however, an inverted watermark occurs as an error, caused by the sheet of paper having been inserted in the printing machine the wrong way up. Conversely there are cases, such as Britain's National Productivity Year, Paris Postal Centenary or Freedom from Hunger stamps of 1962–63, where an inverted watermark is normal.

Perforations

The world's first postage stamps were issued imperforate and had to be cut from the sheet by means of scissors or a sharp knife. In 1848–50 Henry Archer conducted experiments which led to the adoption of perforation in Britain four years later. This convenient method of separation gradually spread to other countries and today it is universally used. However, most countries have released stamps without perforations at some time or another—as a result of war, when the proper machinery was not available, and sometimes deliberately, for sale to collectors. For example, many Communist countries produce limited quantities of stamps without perforations; in France imperforate stamps are presented to postal officials.

In the early days collectors paid little attention to perforations, other than to collect examples of stamps with and without, and some went so far as to trim off the perforations, thinking that the ragged teeth were unsightly! In 1866 the Parisian collector, Dr Legrand, invented an odontometre, or perforation gauge, and from

63 William Wyon's City Medal of 1838. The Queen Victoria profile was drawn by Henry Corbould, and it was used on the Penny Black of 1840 and remained on Great Britain stamps until the Queen's death in 1901

64 Hawaiian typeset 13c 'Missionary' adhesive of 1851, when Hawaii was independent. A good specimen is very valuable

65 The Chalon portrait of Queen Victoria. The full face was used on many British colonial stamps from 1851

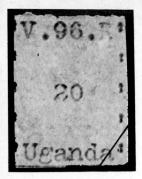

67

66 Uganda 1896 20 cowries stamp typewritten by the Rev Ernest Millar, the missionary
67 A printing flaw in the thistle and rose on cylinder 13 of the British 1½d stamp of 1952 increases its interest and value
68 The famous Great Exhibition held in London in 1851 had many philatelic ramifications. Illustrated is the De la Rue stand

69 A block of eight stamps from the corner of the sheet showing the cylinder numbers, one for each colour used in printing the 5d of Great Britain's 1970 Dickens series

68

then onward the study of perforations has been indispensable. It was discovered that many stamps, apparently identical, had different perforations: either the holes differed in size or the frequency of the holes varied. Dr Legrand's gauge was based on the number of holes in a line two centimetres long. Thus a stamp described as being 'perf 12' would have twelve holes in a space of two centimetres.

In stamp catalogues and lists a stamp is regarded as having the same gauge of perforations on all four sides if only one figure is given. Where the horizontal and vertical perforations are of different gauges, two sets of figures are given. Thus a stamp perf 12×13 would be twelve at the top and bottom and thirteen on the sides.

In true perforation small circles of paper are actually punched out. Another form of separation, in which the paper is merely pierced, is known as rouletting. There are many kinds of roulette, distinguished by the appearance of the cuts made in the paper. Some of the more common forms are roulette in coloured lines (Thurn and Taxis), cross roulette (Madeira), serpentine roulette (Finland) and saw-toothed (Postwar Berlin-Brandenburg). Pin-perforation denotes a type of separation in which the paper is pierced with holes but no paper is removed as in proper perforation. Pin-perforation occurs with a threadless sewing machine. Interrupted perforations occur on stamps from time to time, and can either be accidental (when one or more of the perforating 'teeth' are blunt or broken) or deliberate—for example, certain coil stamps of the Netherlands and Ireland.

The coil stamps of many countries are either horizontally or vertically imperforate. Partial perforation may also occur in stamp booklets where the outer edges of the pane are imperforate either accidentally or deliberately.

Gum

Today most stamps are issued with some sort of gum on the back. The earliest form of adhesive ('cement' they used to call it) was produced from potato starch. A more satisfactory substance is gum arabic and this is now the most widely used fixative. Since 1968, however, the stamps of Great Britain and many Commonwealth countries have used a material known as polyvinyl alcohol (PVA). It is virtually colourless and has the advantage of not causing the paper to curl in poor climatic conditions. The Machin definitives of Great Britain may be found with gum arabic or PVA gum, but obviously this difference is of interest only in mint stamps. Other countries, notably Germany at the end of the Second World War, have made use of different types of gum which are of interest to the specialist, and from Germany comes a curious form of gumming in

70 Tête-bêche pair of Swiss William Tell stamps of 1914 printed by typography

71 An error in recess printing. Falkland Islands 1964 6d with a vignette of HMS *Glasgow* instead of HMS *Kent*

72 The normal Falkland Islands 1964 6d showing HMS *Kent*

73 An outstanding cover. A pair of the British Guiana 2c of 1850, nicknamed 'cottonreels' because of their similarity to the circular labels on reels of cotton

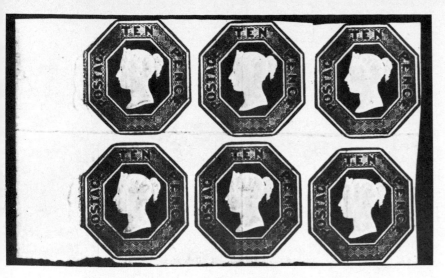

74 Embossing, 1850. The die was engraved at the Royal Mint by William Wyon and the stamps printed at Somerset House. This magnificent block of six is from the Royal Collection

75 A display showing a drawing of an embossing press, dies, and the plaster cast by Edmund Dulac of the head of King George VI from which the dies were made

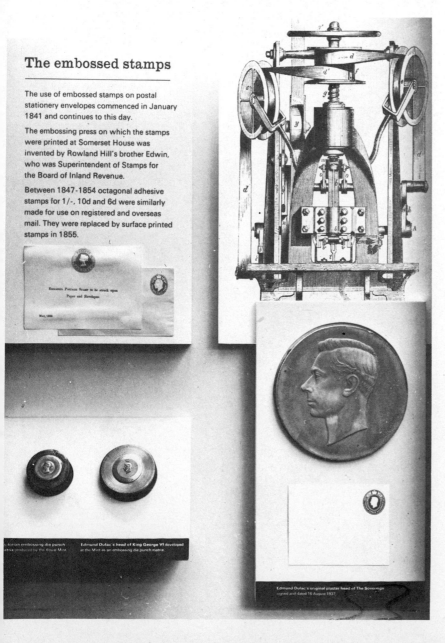

The embossed stamps

The use of embossed stamps on postal stationery envelopes commenced in January 1841 and continues to this day.

The embossing press on which the stamps were printed at Somerset House was invented by Rowland Hill's brother Edwin, who was Superintendent of Stamps for the Board of Inland Revenue.

Between 1847-1854 octagonal adhesive stamps for 1/-, 10d and 6d were similarly made for use on registered and overseas mail. They were replaced by surface printed stamps in 1855.

a pattern of blobs, known as *spargummi* (economy gum).

The fashion for collecting stamps in 'unmounted mint' condition has unfortunately stimulated the fraudulent regumming of stamps. Many of the older stamps were stuck to the album page by means of their own mucilage and could only be removed by soaking them off, thereby losing the gum. Thus classic stamps with full original gum now command a premium and this has encouraged the not so gentle art of regumming. Detection is often difficult, though the fakers seldom manage to get gum of the correct consistency or composition, and there are usually tell-tale brush marks, which may be lacking in the genuine gum.

Methods of printing

Stamps are produced by more than one process, and this may have an important bearing on their value. This tends to happen in a definitive series, especially where the basic stamps are in use over a long period. The Irish definitive series, introduced in 1922—23, was printed by typography. The 3d and 5d stamps, however, were produced in 1966—67 by photogravure and since the entire series was superseded by new designs in 1968 the latter method was of short duration. Eventually the photogravure will be scarcer than the typographed series.

The Austrian definitive series, released at intervals between 1957 and 1968, was printed by various methods. In fact, all four major methods were used at some time or other in the manufacture of these stamps—recess, typography, lithography and photogravure. Fortunately few stamps were printed by more than one process, but those to watch for are the 50 groschen (lithographed or photogravure), the 1 schilling (typographed, lithographed or photogravure) and the 1.50s (lithographed or photogravure). It will then be realised how it is essential to be able to tell the different processes and recognise their characteristics.

Recess

The world's first stamps were recess printed. This process was one in which the early printers, like Perkins Bacon and the American Bank Note Co specialised. Stamps produced in this way are sometimes said to be line-engraved, though this more correctly describes the manufacture of the plate. In this process lines are engraved in the surface of the plate and ink is forced into the resultant grooves or recesses. The paper is moistened and applied to the plate under great pressure, so that it is forced into the grooves where it picks up the ink. Stamps printed in this way have a characteristic ridged impression, which can be seen under a magnifying glass. The process is generally used for British high value stamps. Most French, Canadian and United States stamps have been printed by this method.

76 How a multicoloured stamp is produced by the printing of one colour upon another. Five colours are used on the Grenada 60c stamp of Easter 1970. (This book is not printed in the five actual colours of the stamp so this is an approximate reconstruction). Colour separation on this stamp is the work of Bradbury Wilkinson, stamp producers since 1876

77–79 Three stamps printed by lithography:
77 Gibraltar 2d marking the 20th anniversary of UNESCO
78 The first lithographed stamp, the Zurich issue of 1843
79 30f Iraq of 1966 to mark Mohammed's birthday

80–87 Eight stamps printed by the photogravure method, a widely used technique:
80 6d Fiji of 1964 printed by Harrison and Sons
81 Gibraltar 1966 1d stamp to commemorate Winston Churchill printed by Harrison and Sons
82 2s 'Our Lady of Europa' stamp, issued by Gibraltar in 1966, printed by Harrison and Sons
83 1967 40f stamp of the Malagasy Republic printed by Delrieu
84 9d Malawi definitive printed by Harrison and Sons
85 1953 1a of Macao printed by Courvoisier
86 Ghana 4d definitive printed by Harrison and Sons
87 Iraq Army Day stamp of 1960, showing General Kassem, printed by Courvoisier

77

78

79

80

81

82

83

84

85

86

87

Typography

This is the opposite of recess, in that the plate is cut away from the lines, which take up the ink and press into the paper. Alternative names for this process are surface printing or letterpress. This method was very popular from the 1850s (when De La Rue introduced it) till the 1930s, when it was gradually superseded by photogravure. Its chief merit was its cheapness, since moulds, stereos and electrotypes could be multiplied very easily.

Typography results in a much coarser impression than recess. It can be recognised in many cases by the slight indentation on the backs of the stamps. A variation of this is type-setting, in which printer's type (letters, figures and ornaments) is assembled to form a design. Type-set stamps include the famous Hawaiian Missionaries, the British Guiana Cottonreels, the first stamps of Reunion and the stamps of Tolima.

Lithography

The name is derived from two Greek words— *lithos*, a stone, and *graphein*, to write. In its earliest form a special type of limestone was used in this process. The required impression would be made in fat ink; the stone then wetted and a roller inked over the stone. The fat ink on the roller would be repelled by the wetted portion of the stone, but taken up by the fat ink impression of the drawing. When the paper was placed on the stone, it would take up an impression from the inked area.

Over the years various refinements in the basic process have been evolved, leading to the modern multicolour offset lithographic processes which often go under such names as Duotone Offset (Canada) and Delacryl (a De La Rue patent).

Lithography is characterised by its flat appearance, with neither the ridged effect of recess printing nor the indentation found in typography.

Photogravure

In essence this process, also known as rotogravure or heliogravure, is a form of recess printing produced by a photo-mechanical technique.

An image is transferred photographically on to a coated cylinder, which is then immersed in an acid bath and the image etched into it. This is multiplied the requisite number of times by the 'step and repeat' process in order to build up the printing cylinder.

Photogravure was first used by Bavaria in 1914. Harrison and Sons Ltd used it to print stamps for Egypt (1923) and the Gold Coast (1928) before adopting it for British stamps from 1934 onwards. Photogravure exhibits a fine screen of dots; but it should be noted that modern offset lithography and half-tone typography also show a screening effect.

88 Photography was used to produce the Mafeking Siege stamps of 1900. These locals have great historic interest

89 A modern photogravure error. 1964 Southern Rhodesia 1s stamp with the Queen's portrait and the word 'Emeralds' missing. A sheet of 60 contained 18 such errors

90,91 Sample stamps produced by Waterlow and Sons Ltd were overprinted by the firm's name and the word 'specimen'. The fortifications design for Peru was line perforated. The Venezuela miniature sheet was printed from plates laid down from stamp rollers

Other processes

Apart from the four main processes other methods have been used to print stamps. Embossing was adopted for the British 6d, 10d and 1s stamps of 1847–54, and was popular with many of the old German states in the 1860s. It has a limited application nowadays in the gold-foil embossing of the Queen's profile on many British commemorative stamps. Die-stamping on metal foil has been used to create the gimmicky stamps of Tonga, Bhutan and other countries, already referred to. Photography was used to produce the famous Siege stamps of Mafeking in 1900 and the Figueroa airmail stamp of Chile. Type-written stamps have been issued by Long Island, Uganda and Albania, while some of the postmasters' issues of Germany at the end of the Second World War were produced by duplicating. As a rule these unusual processes are only used in times of emergency.

Further reading

For a general appreciation of stamp production there is nothing better than studying the catalogues, particularly the specialised editions. Here is a straightforward list.

Stanley Gibbons. *Specialised, Great Britain* Vol 1, *Queen Victoria*; Vol 2, *King Edward* VII to *King George* VI; Vol 3, *Queen Elizabeth* II. *British Commonwealth Catalogue*.

Handbook of Irish Philately, David Feldman Ltd and The Dolmen Press Ltd, Dublin.

Switzerland Specialised. The Amateur Collector, London NW8.

Scott. Vol 1, *USA and American*; Vol II, *Rest of the World* (A to J); Vol III, *Rest of the World* (K to Z); *USA Specialised*.

Minkus. *All America*; Vol I, *American and British Commonwealth*; Voll II, *Rest of the World*.

Michel. *Germany Specialised*.

Prinet. *Specialised Catalogue of Belgium*.

Sassone. *Italy and Colonies Specialised*; *Old Italian States*.

Bolaffi. *Italy Specialised*; *Vatican City and Roman States*.

Yvert and Tellier. Vol I, *France and Colonies*; Vol II, *Europe*; Voll III, *Rest of the World*.

Zumstein. *Swiss Specialised*; *Europe*.

For a detailed study of the production of British stamps the reader is strongly advised to consult: *The Postage Stamps of Great Britain* in four volumes, covering all the issues from the early imperforate line-engraved stamps to the modern productions. They are published by The Royal Philatelic Society, 41 Devonshire Place, London W1.

The original Bath mail coach. On the side of the coach can be seen the sign of the Swan with Two Necks in Lad Lane, London, where the coach arrived in the morning after its overnight run from Bath

Stamp collecting as a hobby has been with us for about 120 years, yet basically the methods of collecting have changed little. Stamps are still secured in an album of stout paper leaves, usually by means of gummed hinges, and although in recent years 'slip in' mounting, whereby specimens are merely placed under a clear, protective covering, has gained some popularity, the majority of collectors still prefer to use hinges.

In many other ways, too, collectors have remained conservative: the arrangement of issues, the manner of 'writing up', even the continued preference for popular countries and groups. However, there is one big change that has taken place. As the great general collections of well-known philatelists become broken up in auctions, they are not likely to be replaced: the general collector is disappearing.

The reason for this is simple to explain: too many new issues from too many countries.

For this reason a newcomer to the hobby, unless a young boy or girl, would be well advised to leave general collecting alone. For youngsters, gathering together some of the stamps of the whole world is a good thing, for it makes for an appreciation of philately in general, and has an educational value. But for the adult collector to try to take on the whole world is an impossible task today. If one inherits a big collection or can afford to buy a good, ready-made one, that is a different matter, for this can bridge the gap of many years. There is great joy to be found in building up a large, all-the-world collection; it is rather like gradually, painstakingly fitting in the pieces of a gigantic jigsaw puzzle.

Album publishers still cater for the general collector, but although there are hundreds for the beginner, only a few are produced for the serious collector, such as Stanley Gibbons Commonwealth 'Imperial' (1840–1936), 'King George VI' (1952) and 'New Age' (Elizabethan), and the giant 'Global' of Minkus of America. Unless a general collection is being added to steadily, it is apt to look lost in these big albums, and of course if the owner decides to sell, it at once becomes apparent that a scattered collection does not command a good price—unless it contains many complete sets and a smattering of 'earlies'.

Most adult collectors today concentrate on a small group of countries or specialise in one particular country. The choice is wide, and album publishers now produce many excellent one-country albums, like the 'Collecta' series. If the idea is to specialise 'in depth' then an interesting country with a high potential should be chosen. Such countries are Great Britain, Canada, France, Germany, Union of South Africa and USA, which have everything to offer, although being so popular it is sometimes

92 The first designs for the Bangladesh stamps; they differ slightly from the issued set

93 A new country entered the stamp album on 29 July 1971: Bangladesh. Eight definitive postage stamps were issued and here the Bengalee designer Biman Mullick (left) and Ambassador Abu Sayeed Chowdhury (centre) show the designs to the Rt Hon John Stonehouse, MP, a former Postmaster General

94 A print of 1852 showing a mail train guard supervising the loading of luggage before the train's departure. The railway is the London and North-Western Railway, on which mail was carried from Euston Station, London, every evening. About 17 tons of mail was carried daily at the beginning of this railway's service in the middle of the 19th century

Plate 5.   Red. Registered 1.6.40

Frame lines often weak. N.E. square frequently defective. Unit value in black 12.

Plate 8.   Red. Registered 31.7.40

O flaw.

Unit value in black 14.

Plate 10.   Red. Registered 2.12.40

O flaw. J. square-footed Distinctive grey Unit value in black 60.

96

95 The Penny Black with 'VR' in the top corner was prepared in 1840, intended for official use, but was not used

96 1840 Penny Blacks and 1841 Penny Reds printed from the same plate

97 Control letter and number on the margin of a sheet of 1½d George V definitive of Great Britain

98

98 Imperforate Twopenny Blues. They were separated by cutting with scissors

99 An 1884 4d Victorian definitive

100 An 1887 6d Queen Victoria Jubilee issue

101 Queen Victoria 4d Jubilee issue of 1887

hard to find a new approach in specialisation. All the big groups are well provided with literature—handbooks and specialised catalogues; for this reason many collectors in search of a country are seeking adventure with one that is smaller or less popular, perhaps combining two or three together.

It is always an advantage, before deciding on a particular country, to read at least one book on the subject. By doing this its possibilities should be revealed—the postal history prospects, the historical and geographical background, the scope for study in the old and the new issues, the interest in the actual designs, the hope of completing sets without too heavy a financial outlay—this question of cost will be shown in the catalogue.

To assist the reader, some useful books and essential catalogues appertaining to the groups are listed after each resumé.

Great Britain

This group has *everything*: early and modern postal history; prestamp covers; postage stamps and postal stationery from 1840 spanning the reigns of six great monarchs; inland revenues; officials; local carriage and railway labels; postage dues; air stamps; booklets—you name it, Great Britain has it.

A sensible approach to a country with so much to offer the would-be specialist is first to become well conversant with the postage stamps. The Penny Black should start off the line-engraved issues of 1840. This famous stamp can be an extensive study on its own, but that form of specialisation is for the person with plenty of money available for such things. The companion Twopenny Blue is another 'gem', and as both these early masterpieces in miniature are such a gilt-edge investment, a collector would be well advised to acquire them before they increase in price, even though it might mean ignoring all the following issues until enough funds are available for the purchase of the world's first two stamps. Once these 'kingpins' are safely in place, then the following issues will gradually find their way into the album.

What price to pay for the pair? A used Penny Black with white margins on four sides—that is, the frame design not snipped into by careless Victorian scissors—should cost about £8 ($25 Scott), and a used Twopenny Blue, also showing margins round the design, about £18 ($55 Scott). As with all classics, condition plays a very important part in the pricing; the above figures refer to good average copies.

The change of colour to red-brown for the 1d and the white lines added above and below the portrait of the 2d blue in 1841 are an interesting pair, with plenty of varieties, including the Maltese Cross obliterations with numbers (1 to 12) in the Cross.

102,103 A few sheets of the 1881 1d lilac and the 1887 ½d vermilion were overprinted on the back PEAR'S SOAP as an advertisement for the famous soap manufacturers. The Postmaster General objected, and this form of advertising was abandoned

104 An enlargement of the engraving on the die from which the famous Great Britain Penny Black of 1840 was printed. Of course, the image is reversed during the process of printing.

105 A block of 33 Penny Blacks showing re-entry on AD and double letter on DG

106–109 The pictorial high values of the Great Britain issue of 1951:
106 The 2/6 value shows HMS *Victory*
107 The 5s value shows the white cliffs of Dover
108 The 10s value shows St George and the dragon
109 The £1 value shows the Royal Coat of Arms

106

107

108

109

110–113 British polar explorers for the Great Britain issue of 1972:
110 The 3p value shows James Clark Ross
111 The 5p value shows Martin Frobisher
112 The 7½p value shows Henry Hudson
113 The 9p value shows Robert Falcon Scott

110

111

112

113

The perforated 1d and 2d stamps that followed will also give the student opportunities for research work, and when the 1864 Penny Reds with letters in the four corners are tackled, the chase will be on, for there are 152 individual plate numbers to be found in the centre of the spandrels on both sides of the portrait. These numbers from 71 to 225 are certainly worth looking for. Most of them are on specimens that are inexpensive (used), but if during the search a 225 turns up, then an item catalogued at £20 ($65 Scott) has been discovered. Should Lady Luck be in a really good mood and plate no. 77 is discovered, the fortunate finder has hit the jack-pot with a specimen catalogued at £2,250 ($7,500 Scott).

Britain's smallest stamp, the ½d rose of 1870, is worthy of more attention than it normally gets. Here there are fifteen plate numbers to collect, imperforate specimens and watermark varieties to search out.

The last stamp in this line-engraved series was the attractive 1½d red with the shield border round Victoria's portrait. Catalogued at £1 ($2 Scott), this is a stamp which has an investment potential, and there is an error well-worth the finding—the letters in the four corners showing OP—PC instead of CP—PC, which sends an unused specimen normally catalogued at £5 ($12.50) shooting up to £275 ($750) and used up to £45 ($165).

The embossed 6d, 10d and 1s of 1847—54 have never been over popular, which is a good reason for taking them up as a study.

The surface-printed issues of 1855—92 are a big group that make an interesting study, with all the variations of printing, shades, perforations, watermarks so dear to the heart of the true specialist.

The Edwardians of 1901—10 are a short, compact section with only 16 designs (½d to £1) including the 2d Tyrian Plum, which was never issued to the public; its value today is about £3,000.

The King George V series of 1910—36 contains some fine designs, such as the high value 'Seahorses' of 1913—18, the 1924—25 British Empire Exhibition Wembley 'Lions' (which appear to increase in value each year), and the finest £1 design so far produced—issued to commemorate the Ninth Universal Postal Union Congress of 1929.

The brief reign of King Edward VIII (20 January to 10 December 1936) produced four values in a simple, yet bold design.

For the coronation of King George VI and Queen Elizabeth (the Queen Mother) a single specimen was produced in 1936, followed by a definitive series and a number of special issues, including a lovely blue £1 for the Royal Silver Wedding.

Queen Elizabeth II ascended the throne on

114 The unique King Edward VII 2d Tyrian Plumb of May, 1910. Although prepared for use, it was never issued, and is very valuable

115 A block of four 1912 1½d King George V definitives of Great Britain with a flaw on the bottom right stamp, PENCF being printed for PENCE

116 The red arrow shows the 'Devil's Horn' variety on a 1934 King George V photogravure stamp. Found on cylinder 36, 12th specimen on the first row
117 The £1 value from the Ninth Universal Postal Union Congress commemorative set of Great Britain, 1929, one of the finest £1 values so far produced

6 February 1952, and in 1952–54 a national emblems definitive set appeared. From Her Majesty's coronation in 1953, when four special stamps appeared, the stamp issuing policy of the General Post Office altered radically: 1955 saw the appearance of four high values showing famous castles, and then from 1957 they abandoned the time-honoured policy of restraint and treated—if that is the word—collectors to a bonanza of pictorials. Events, both prominent and not so prominent, crowded in on one another to be recognised philatelically. Even the Scots were appeased at last with a Skirving chalk drawing and the Nasmyth portrait of Robert Burns, each on a value to commemorate the great bard.

England's World Cup football victory that sent most Englishmen wild with excitement in 1966 had a special stamp, and even another battle fought 900 years previously—the Battle of Hastings—commemorated two months after the World Cup with eight scenes of slaughter, failed to arouse the same enthusiasm as the Wembley battle. Then two Christmas stamps were also issued in 1966, which were Britain's first contribution to the fast-growing subject of Christmas issues of the world.

But while the many and varied pictorials form an extensive group, it is the Arnold Machin portrait definitives of 1967 onwards that constitute an ideal study for the philatelist.

The Machin definitives are so called because the portrait was taken from a plaster cast prepared by the sculptor Arnold Machin, who was also responsible for the final stamp design. The simplicity of the design, incorporating as it does just the portrait and denomination, has captured the attention—and admiration—of many people.

For those wishing to specialise, this issue offers many possibilities on account of the changes, made to correspond with adjusted postage rates, and the growth of mechanisation in the Post Office.

The series has a common design, the small lower values printed in photogravure by Harrison and Sons Limited, the larger high values recess printed by Bradbury Wilkinson and Co Ltd.

The '£sd' series was issued in stages starting on 5 June 1967 with the 4d, 1s and 1s 9d values, and ending on 5 March 1969 with the 2s 6d–£1 values.

All the low value stamps were intended to be phosphor lined for use with the automatic letter facing machinery, but all values have been found with the phosphor omitted, the quantities involved varying considerably. Most values have two phosphor bands (although denominations up to 4d also exist with just one band) normally placed centrally down the stamp, although occasionally to the right or

118 The 1½d value of the Great Britain British Empire Exhibition issue of 1924

119 King George VI stamp of Great Britain, 1937, showing the control letter and year digits in the fractional control. The smaller figures, 24, indicate the cylinder number

120 Tête-bêche of King George VI definitive issue
121 The 'Phantom R' in the Jubilee line in the margin of a sheet of Great Britain's 1960 3d issue

left of the stamp from certain stamp booklets. As an experiment the 1s 6d value was released on 10 December 1969 with an all-over phosphor coating in place of the normal phosphor bands.

The first £sd values to be issued (3d, 4d sepia, 9d, 1s, 1s 6d and 1s 9d) were printed on paper with the natural gum arabic, which has a shiny appearance. Because stocks of gum arabic became unavailable the printers had to develop a synthetic adhesive, known to collectors as polyvinyl alcohol gum, which has a dull appearance. All the subsequent Machin definitives were printed on paper with PVA gum, with one or two exceptions. These were the 4d printed in red, which was found in certain 6s booklets with gum arabic, and the se-tenant strips of 2d-2d-3d-1d-4d, available from stamp machines, which were also printed on paper with gum arabic.

In September of 1968 it was decided to introduce a two-tier letter system (i.e. first and second class mail) in Great Britain. The two rates at the time were 5d for first class mail and 4d for second class mail. At the time of introduction the 4d was printed in sepia and the 5d in deep blue, two colours which are not easily distinguished in artificial light. It was therefore decided to change the colour of the 4d to red, and at the same time change the 8d, which had previously itself been red, to pale blue. The new colours were issued on 6 January 1969.

Apart from the missing phosphor varieties already mentioned, a few other errors have been noted on these stamps. The 1s 6d, normally printed in deep blue and turquoise blue, was found with the latter colour omitted. The 10d value, and the panes of stamps from the £1 'Stamps for Cooks' booklets, were found printed on paper lacking the normal coating. Imperforate stamps from sheets, booklets and rolls were found, in addition to a 4d sepia tête-bêche pair.

Towards the end of the life of the £sd stamps, a cylinder number was introduced for the cylinder which printed the phosphor ink. This took the form of a 'Ph1' which appeared somewhere in the right-hand sheet margin of sheets of the 2d, 5d, 6d, 7d and 9d values which showed the normal cylinder number followed by a full stop. The normal cylinder number as usual appeared alongside the 18th or 19th row of stamps in the left-hand margin.

The low value decimal stamps were issued on 15 February 1971, although the postal strike at the time meant that many areas did not receive their supplies until March, when the strike finished. The high values had been issued earlier, namely on 17 June 1970. Because the £1 remained the basic unit, this value did not change, although it was now printed in sheets

122–124 The Great Britain Christmas stamps of 1968, designed by Rosalind Dease, showed children playing with their toys

125,126 The Queen Elizabeth design of the 1967 Great Britain stamps has the dignified simplicity of the 1840 Penny Black. The design is from a plaster cast by Arnold Machin

127 This Great Britain Paintings stamp, showing Constable's 'The Hay Wain' has an error: the gold has been omitted which normally shows the value, 1/9, and the Queen's head

of 100 as opposed to sheets of 40 for the earlier printings.

Phosphor cylinder numbers were introduced on all the low values, now appearing in the left margins of all sheets. However, the printers at first experimented with the exact nature of these numbers, details of which can be found in the specialised catalogues.

All the low values had two phosphor bands, except the 2½p which had only one.

The 10p was originally recess printed on paper with an all-over phosphor coating, but subsequently changed to the small photogravure format. This latter stamp was printed in two colours, orange and pale orange, and has been found with the pale orange omitted.

It is hoped that this brief resumé of the Machin definitives will indicate what an excellent choice it offers for specialisation, enabling the collector to make many finds himself—at face value from the local post office!

Booklets

One aspect of collecting which has become more popular during the currency of the Machin definitives is the interest in stamp booklets. This has developed as a result of the decision by the Post Office to release stamp booklets with pictorial covers, the design of the covers being changed at regular intervals. Such covers were introduced on 23 March 1968.

Considerable enthusiasm was shown for the experimental £1 booklet released on 1 December 1969. In place of the usual advertisement interleaving pages, this booklet contained recipes and consequently was known as the 'Stamps for Cooks' booklet. It was larger than normal, containing panes of 15 stamps which were attached to a tab bearing part of the recipe. Of particular note was the se-tenant pane containing three rows of 4d-1d-5d-1d-4d, although it should be pointed out that se-tenant panes had appeared in earlier and later booklets.

With the introduction of decimal currency it was considered desirable that stamp booklets should maintain the same format as before, with the stamps being contained therein in multiples of five. For this reason most of the decimal stamp booklet panes incorporated advertisement labels.

Many collectors are specialising in stamp booklets, since varieties can be found in the style of binding, the method of perforation, and the screen of the phosphor bands. Further details of these can be found in specialised catalogues.

Besides the normal pictorial variety, stamp booklet covers have been used to publicise the International Stamp Exhibition, Philympia 1970 and the '80 Years of Stamp Books' exhibition during 1971 at the National Postal Museum, London.

128–132 In 1969 Great Britain commemorated notable anniversaries with a special issue. Two values celebrate aviation 'firsts' of fifty years earlier, other values recognise organisations

Special albums for booklets are now published, and these make the items displayed in them very attractive, especially the pictorial covers.

The lure of Elizabethans

If you were to ask British stamp dealers which is the most popular modern collecting group, they would answer—Queen Elizabeth II.

The reasons seem to be obvious enough. Naturally interest in the British Commonwealth is strongest in the British Isles, and these stamps are relatively easy to obtain. This is particularly true of the more recent issues.

However, ease of securing supplies is not the sole criterion to ensure popularity. There must still be a basic attractiveness about the stamps themselves.

It is in this respect that the Commonwealth issues really score. The Commonwealth spans the globe, and likewise the stamps reflect different climes, cultures, races and religions. But let us look at the lure of Elizabethan stamps rather more closely.

As stated in another Chapter, thematic or topical collecting has become very popular everywhere. Elizabethan stamp designs will supply such collectors with almost every subject they need.

Many of the Commonwealth countries have released stamps featuring their wild life: birds, fishes, animals, and so on. Other subjects which have appeared include aircraft, sailing vessels, tourist attractions. Modern printing techniques have ensured that realistic illustrations can be achieved at postage stamp size.

As mentioned earlier, being scattered throughout the World, the Commonwealth offers the possibility of many different area groupings. The Pacific Islands have always been a popular group, possibly because of their romantic settings. The Atlantic islands offer dreams of a desert island existence. Africa provides examples of the progress of civilisation, as emergent nations gain independence, and although some of the African issues are a little flamboyant, they have a fresh look that draws attention to their message of freedom.

It is natural that as each nation strives to carve out its own existence in this competitive world and strives to establish its name among the World leaders, it sees that the medium of postage stamps are ideal ambassadors, ideal means for propaganda. Thus stamps can be relied upon to reflect current World events, both in subject matter and style.

For any collector embarking on a Commonwealth collection, a look through a stamp catalogue will soon give an indication of which stamps are likely to have the greatest appeal. But we must not assume that this appeal will be based solely on design.

Stamp printing has advanced considerably during the past few years. At the start of the

133 Stamps booklets containing stamps of various denominations are sold in British Post Offices

134 An unaccepted design for the investiture of HRH The Prince of Wales issue of 1969

135 1d Guernsey stamp of 1941

reign of Queen Elizabeth II most stamps were either recess printed, in one or possibly two colours, or printed in one colour photogravure. Today, lithography is used to a great extent, producing full colour effects, while photogravure is being continually perfected. In addition, new ideas have been developed, such as self-adhesive stamps of Sierra Leone and Tonga which, while not appealing to all collectors, have attracted publicity and new recruits to the hobby.

Printing considerations have meant that changes have occurred in the watermarks and perforations of stamps, while in recent years the paper used for printing has been modified so that one paper may be suitable for all printing processes. Even the gum on the backs of stamps has changed from the natural gum arabic to a synthetic adhesive.

Many collectors find studying these changes of great interest, particularly as a new printing of a basic stamp can often result in a change in shade for one or more of the colours in which it is printed.

However, other considerations can also affect the printing of stamps. More and more countries are finding that automation is the only way to cut costs. Stamps in many ways reflect this trend, being issued in modified form for use with automatic equipment.

Thus it is easily seen that a fascinating collection can be built up simply by analysing the changes that occur as a result of progress in printing techniques and automation. Even changes in postage rates, which is an increasing burden throughout the World, can offer scope for specialisation.

The simple fact is that whatever form one wishes the stamp collection to take, it can be achieved through the realm of Queen Elizabeth II British Commonwealth issues. And in the main the majority of these stamps are inexpensive—always an important consideration when a group is an extensive one.

While it is not intended to enter into a discussion on stamp investment, it is true that with the volume of new stamps being released, coupled with a consistent demand, most dealers are finding they are unable to put aside large stocks for future sales. Consequently, supplies of obsolete stamps are often not available to satisfy the never-ending demand. Thus, a collector who builds up a fine collection should not be too disappointed when the time comes to sell. One piece of advice here: always try to get the high values of a set. They may be expensive and it might mean buying fewer incomplete sets in order to afford the top values, but should the time come when the collection has to be sold, the sets that are complete are going to fetch a good price.

Apart from the Elizabethans already men-

136–139 These designs by Rosalind Dease were for a suggested series of English historical costumes

tioned under Great Britain, Australia, Canada and New Zealand, some of the smaller groups have great attraction.

The Regional issues of Isle of Man, Northern Ireland, Scotland, Wales and Monmouthshire, together with the Channel Islands of Guernsey and Jersey and their interesting stamp booklets, make a most attractive showing. A glance through one of the special Elizabethan catalogues will show some of the great possibilities of these modern issues from Aden on the south coast of Arabia, Anguilla and Antigua of the Leeward Islands, Ascension in the South Atlantic, and Bahamas in the British West Indies, to the romantic pictorials of Pitcairn Islands in the Pacific Ocean, and the story of the mutineers and the *Bounty* which has been so dramatically told in film and book.

In this reign the stamps of the Commonwealth have produced designs that, for beauty of colour, interest and novelty can match anything that other countries produce.

Further Reading

The Elizabethan era is well provided for in reference works.

British Elizabethan Stamps by David Potter. B. T. Batsford Ltd, London W1, 1971.

The Commonwealth Queen Elizabeth II Stamp Catalogue, 1972. Urch, Harris and Co Ltd, Bristol.

Commonwealth Q.E.II, 1972. John Lister, London SW1.

Elizabethan Stamp Catalogue, 1972. Stanley Gibbons, London WC2.

Simplified Catalogue of Varieties on Queen Elizabeth Postage Stamps, 1968. Shelly Stamps, London EC4.

The Woodstock Catalogue of British Elizabethan Stamps, 1970–71. The Woodstock Catalogue Co Ltd, London WC2.

140 First day cover showing the British ships issue of 1969 including the 9d Cutty Sark

Australia

It must not be thought that because the Commonwealth of Australia is a 'new' country it does not possess an early philatelic background. Although formed in 1901 as an independent member of the Commonwealth, the early issues of this immense island continent reach right back to within ten years of the world's first postage stamp.

A little of the antique background of Australian stamps may be gathered from the following:

Victoria, 1850–1910. The well-known 'Half-Length' portrait of Queen Victoria, together with the 'Queen on Throne' have given distinction to this former British colony's issues. The British general catalogue has made the stamps an ideal hunting ground for the technically minded enthusiast, but a complicated off-putting listing for the newcomer. The 1873–84 set contains one of the smallest stamps issued, the half-penny rose-red (shades), issued also in 1901 in blue-green (shades). Other interesting stamps were those showing coins (1870, 1884, 1897) and the most famous of all war medals, the Victoria Cross, awarded for conspicuous gallantry in the Boer War 1900 (1d stamp of May 1900 sold at 1s each for a Patriotic Fund).

New South Wales, 1850–1910. From this land in the South Pacific Ocean came the famous 'Sydney Views', the first issues showing the Seal of the Colony.

Tasmania, 1853–1913. From the first crude issues of 'Van Diemens Land' to the 1899 pictorial designs—among the earliest of scenic issues—there is a wealth of material available, at a reasonable price. But once 'discovered' by the modern collector in search of an old, unspoilt country, prices could start moving up rapidly. The name of the island was changed on the stamps from Van Diemens Land to Tasmania in 1858.

Western Australia, 1854–1912. Famed for the 'Black Swan' design. The aquatic bird was a feature of nearly all issues, including the large postal fiscals of 1893–99.

South Australia, 1855–1912. Apart from the quite handsome first recess printed series, there are no famous issues here. The 1883 values contain a tiny halfpenny like that of Victoria. There is an imposing list in the catalogues of departmentals—initials on stamps of 1868–74 for various government offices, such as CD (Convict Department), LA (Lunatic Asylum), and from 1874 to 1901 contemporary stamps were overprinted OS, of which there are a number of types and numerous varieties.

Queensland, 1860–1912. New South Wales stamps were used from 26 January to 1 November 1860 and are included in the group if they bear a Queensland postmark. The

142 Victoria also issued one of the smallest stamps, the half-penny of 1874

141 The one-penny 'coin' stamp of 1897 is one of the largest stamps issued during the reign of Victoria; it sold for a shilling, the balance going to a hospital fund

143 The first issue of the Commonwealth of Australia, the 1913 Map and Kangaroo design of B. Young, engraved by S. Reading and printed by typography by J. B. Cooke

144 The Australian Kangaroo of 1913 reappeared in a new setting on this 1938 issue

145 Issued for the first England–Australia flight by Ross and Keith Smith this miniature sheet is worth several hundred pounds and the stamp is listed in an American airmail catalogue at $750 used

famous Chalon Head of Queen Victoria makes the first issues outstanding.

The six former Colonies have been singled out for special mention because it is felt that they offer good prospects for the collector in search of stability. Many of the issues are classics in the true sense, yet quite a number of them are very reasonably priced, when one considers their pedigree.

In 1901 the above six colonies formed the Commonwealth of Australia and in January 1913 the famous Map and Kangaroo issues came out. This, and the King George V design of 1913–36, form one of the finest studies one can have of printing, papers, shades, water-marks. Fortunately the complications are clearly explained in the Australian specialised catalogue, noted in the list of books that follow. Australia has a fine record for interesting designs and short sets, making it an ideal country for the modern collector.

The Australian Post Office is making every effort to popularise its stamps at home and abroad. Well produced publicity material is sent free to collectors on request: Head-quarters, 199 William St., Melbourne, Victoria.

Further Reading

The Australian Commonwealth Specialists' Catalogue. The Hawthorn Press, Melbourne, Annually.

The Australian Stamp Catalogue. Review Publications Pty Ltd, 1972.

The Australian Dependencies Stamp Catalogue. Review Publications Pty, Ltd, Sterling St, Dubbo, NSW, Australia, 1966 (new edition due)

The Stamps of the Commonwealth of Australia (Decimal currency). Alec A. Rosenblum, Melbourne, Australia, 1968.

The External Airmails of Australia by N. C. Baldwin. Francis J. Field Ltd, Sutton Coldfield, England, 1965.

Australian Postage Stamps by P. Collas. The Jacaranda Press, published in the UK by Newnes, 1966.

Australian Postage Stamps. The Early Federal Period 1901 to 1912. Australian Post Office, 1971.

Australian Postage Stamps. The 1913–14 Recess printed series and the King George V Sideface and Pictorial Definitive stamps. Australian Post Office, 1971.

Australian Stamp Collecting by Ian F. Finlay. Lansdowne Press Pty Ltd, Melbourne, 1971.

Rare Australian Stamps by Mark Franklin. A. H. and A. Reed, 51 Whiting St, Artarmon, Sydney, Australia, 1968.

The Stamps of Papua and New Guinea by Mark Franklin. A. H. and A. Reed, Sydney, 1970.

146 A cover addressed to Rochester, England, postmarked Rochester, Australia. The 'Bertram Atlantis Expedition' toured Australia in a seaplane called 'Atlantis', unofficially carrying mail. Some letters inadvertently languished in the Berlin Post Office for five years before being sent to London. The Australian postmark is December 7, 1932; the back has a London postmark, December 8, 1937. It was delivered with an official letter from the postal authorities

147 Western Australia's first issue, the 'Black Swan'

148–151 Four Australia Christmas stamps, from the years 1957, 1958, 1959 and 1971. Australia has produced some of the finest stamps depicting the Christmas theme

148

149

150

151

152

153

154

155

156

157

158

159

160

161

162

163

164

165

166

152 The 1913 King George V Australian 1d stamp
153 The Parliament House at Canberra is featured on this 1927 Australian issue
154 This 5d provisional surcharge on the Australia 4½d value appeared in 1930
155 1934 Australian 1s 6d airmail stamp shows Hermes, the messenger of the Gods
156 The 150th anniversary of New South Wales was celebrated on this 1937 Australian stamp
157, 158 The Australian definitives of 1937 show Queen Elizabeth on the 1d stamp and King George VI on the 2d stamp
159 The 1d green of 1940 showed the Australian Imperial Forces
160 The Duke and Duchess of Gloucester are on this Australian issue of 1945
161 The 150th anniversary of Newcastle, New South Wales, was commemorated on a 1947 Australian issue
162 Australian 'One Pound Jimmy' Aborigine of 1950

163 King George VI Australian issue of 1950
164 Strip of 3½d values of 1953 Australian series featuring beef, butter and wheat
165 Head of Queen Elizabeth II on Australia 3½d deep green of 1959
166 2d value of the Olympic Games series. The Games were held in Australia in 1956, and the stamp was issued in blue in 1954 and green in 1955

Canada

Whoever 'takes on' this exciting country is assured of a task so all-embracing that it will provide pleasure for a lifetime.

Obviously the group has to be divided into sections, otherwise it becomes too scattered for methodical study and display. These sections are clear-cut, so that the collector can concentrate on one at a time and eventually link them up into a compact whole.

Before being absorbed into the Confederation of Canada, the following provinces had an independent issue of stamps:

New Brunswick, 1851–63
Nova Scotia, 1851–63
Prince Edward Island, 1861–72
British Columbia and *Vancouver Islands*, 1860–71. These colonies were united on 19 November 1866 under the name British Columbia. There are three listed stamps for British Columbia and Vancouver Island (1860) and thirteen including surcharges for British Columbia. All are quite expensive.

Newfoundland, 1857–1947. This former dominion contains a number of great rarities in its air section; the early and following issues are mostly 'royalist'. Although joined to the Confederation of Canada on 1 April 1949 and from then ceasing to have its own stamps, Newfoundland is still very popular as a separate group.

With Canadian issues division can be made as follows:

Colony of Canada, 1851–64. Beaver, Prince Albert, Queen Victoria, Jacques Cartier designs —nearly all are scarce items and are best left alone until the issues of the Dominion are well represented in the album.

Dominion of Canada. The 'large type' portrait of Queen Victoria was used for the first emissions of 1868. The Jubilee 16-value set of 1897 is one to try to build up, and the following 'Christmas' stamp celebrating Imperial Penny Postage can make a good little study, although there was only one value (2 cents).

Edward VII, 1903–12. Only one definitive set of 7 values to find, but not easy to complete. The Quebec Tercentenary set of 8 should be completed as soon as possible, for the highest value (20 cents) is difficult to obtain.

George V, 1912–36. The early 'Admiral' and the War Tax issues are an important field for study.

George VI, 1937–52. Quite easy to complete. Coil and booklet issues could be added to boost up this simple group.

Elizabeth II, 1953. The first portraits were not inspiring, but the following designs are full of interest. Canada is determined to attract the collector and the new issues being produced are eye-catching and the thematic collector draws heavily on these for numerous subjects.

167 A magnificent pair of the Canadian twelve pence black of 1851
168 The heraldic flowers of the United Kingdom on the Newfoundland one shilling recess of 1857

169 The first Christmas stamp of Canada, the Map stamp of 1898

170 The 3 cents Canadian King George V stamp of 1935

171 The 3 cents Canadian King George VI stamp of 1937

Anyone seriously interested in Canadian stamps should consider joining the Canadian Philatelic Society of Great Britain (Secretary: Dr C. W. Hollingsworth, 17 Mellish Road, Walsall, Staffs.); an excellent journal, *Maple Leaves*, is published.

Further Reading

The Encyclopaedia of British Empire Postage Stamps, Vol 5, North America. (Canada, Newfoundland; Panama to Alaska). Robson Lowe Ltd, 50 Pall Mall, London SW1. (Due late 1972).

Canadian Roller Cancellations 1894–1930 by E. A. Smythies. Canadian Philatelic Society of Great Britain. 1969.

The First Decimal Issue of Canada 1859–1868 by Geoffrey Whitworth. Royal Philatelic Society. 1969.

The Forwarding Agents by Kenneth Rowe. Robson Lowe Ltd. 1969.

Netto Catalogue 1970 Postage Stamps of Australia and Canada. 98 Queen's Road, Brighton.

172 The Canadian 1935 Princess Elizabeth I cent stamp

173 Canadian $1 War Effort issue of 1942 shows a destroyer
174 The 1951 4c Canadian stamp showing Princess Elizabeth and the Duke of Edinburgh

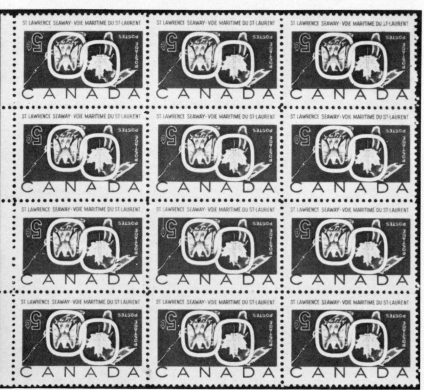

175 A valuable block of twelve of the 1959 Canadian stamps to commemorate the opening of the St Lawrence Seaway. The stamps have their centres inverted and each is catalogued at several hundred pounds. This block was in the first stamp auction to be held at sea, by Robson Lowe on board the *Queen Mary* 16 May 1966

176 From tree to paper, a Canadian 1952 stamp

177 The Charles Connell, the 1860 5c stamp of New Brunswick. Connell was the Postmaster General
178 A unique cover, with overprinted Caribou stamps. The stamps were overprinted for use on mail to be carried by Henry Hawker and Kenneth Mackenzie Grieve on a non-stop flight across the Atlantic in 1919. The aircraft came down in the sea. Only 200 stamps were overprinted, and they are very valuable
179 A first day cover showing the Canadian Christmas stamps of 1968

178

179

180 First day cover of the Canadian Quebec Conference Centenary of 1964

180

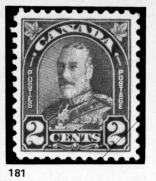

181

182

183

184

185

186

181 The Canadian 2c definitive stamp of 1930—31 shows the head of King George V
182 The Canadian 12c definitive stamp of 1930—31 shows the old citadel at Quebec
183 The 1931 Canadian 10c stamp shows Sir Georges Etienne Cartier
184 The 2c King George V definitive Canadian stamp of 1932—33
185 A panoramic view of Parliament Buildings, Ottawa is shown on this 1933 5c Canadian stamp
186 Jacques Cartier is shown on 1934 3c Canadian stamp to commemorate the fourth centenary of the discovery of Canada in 1534
187 An early George V stamp, a Canadian 2c
188 The yacht *Britannia* is shown on the 13c value of the Canadian Jubilee issue of 1935
189 The Canadian Silver Jubilee issue of 1935 showed several members of the Royal Family. This 5c portrays the Prince of Wales, later the Duke of Windsor

187

188

189

190

191

192

193

194

190 Canadian 4c stamp of 1949 showing Cabot's ship *Matthew*

191 Canadian stamp: Canada geese. The 1946 7c issue
192 The founding of Halifax, Nova Scotia, 200 years earlier is commemorated on the 1949 4c Canadian stamp
193 The Eskimo hunter, the 1955 Canadian 10c definitive
194 Ice hockey is shown on the 5c Canadian commemorative issue of 1956

New Zealand

This country has everything to offer the advanced philatelist, the medium collector and the beginner. From the beautiful Chalon Head of Queen Victoria of 1855 to the modern pictorials there is a wealth of material available for deep study, or just the 'one of each' type of collection.

The Victorian issues that followed the long series of Chalon Head were not brilliantly conceived, in fact the 1873 ½d 'Newspaper Postage' is quite an ugly little stamp, yet the printings on paper watermarked NZ and also without watermark are rising in price.

The interesting pictorials of 1898 are, like many New Zealand designs, overcrowded. The most eagerly awaited sets each year are the Health stamps, first issued in 1929, and the beautiful Christmas stamps, each design from a famous religious painting.

The New Zealand group includes special issues for famous Antarctic expeditions: Shackleton—King Edward VIII Land, and Scott—Victoria Land.

British Possessions under New Zealand control are Aitutaki, Niue, Penrhyn Island, Ross Dependency, for which there are overprinted New Zealand stamps and specially designed issues.

Further reading

Catalogue of the Stamps of New Zealand. Verne, Collins and Co Ltd, Christchurch, New Zealand.

Postage Stamps of New Zealand. Pim and Co (NZ) Ltd, 293 Queen Street, Auckland, and GB Philatelic Publishing Co, 98 Queens Road, Brighton BN1 3YG

The New Zealand Stamp Catalogue. Review Publications Pty Ltd, Sterling St, Dubbo, NSW, Australia, 1970.

New Zealand. The Great Barrier Island 1898—99 Pigeon Post Stamps by J. Reg Walker. The Collectors Club, 22 East 35th Street, New York, NY 10016, USA, 1968.

Historic Place Names of New Zealand by L. S. Rickard. Minerva Ltd, 13 Commerce Street, Auckland.

The External Air Mails of New Zealand (1928—63) by N. C. Baldwin. Francis J. Field Ltd, Sutton Coldfield, England.

King George VI Coil Stamps. Claud Scott. Agent: Campbell Paterson Ltd, PO Box 5555, Auckland, 1970.

195

196

197

195 1943 New Zealand stamp showing Princess Elizabeth
196 New Zealand Health stamp of 1952 showing Prince Charles: 2d is for postage, 1d for health
197 New Zealand Health stamp of 1953 showing boy scouts. The morse code message round the edge reads 'Health' along the top and bottom, and 'New Zealand' on both sides

198

199

200

201

202

198 1958 New Zealand Hawke's Bay Centennial stamp showing sheep shearing
199 Hawke's Bay Centennial stamp of 1958 showing the statue 'Pania'
200 New Zealand 1958 stamp celebrating the 30th anniversary of the first Tasman flight by Sir Charles Kingsford Smith
201 Hawke's Bay Centennial Stamp of 1958 showing gannets
202 New Zealand Health stamp of 1960 showing a wood pigeon

203

204

205

206

205,206 Prince Andrew on two values, 2½d and 3d, of the New Zealand Health Stamps of 1963

207 New Zealand 3d stamp of 1963 to commemorate the centenary of railways

208 Brown trout on the New Zealand 7½c of 1967

209

210

211

209–211 New Zealand armed forces stamps of 1968:
209 Army 4c stamp
210 Air Force 10c stamp
211 Navy 28c stamp

212–216 Butterflies and moths set of New Zealand, 1970:
212 1c value shows Red Admiral butterfly
213 2c value shows Tussock butterfly
214 2½c value shows Magpie moth
215 3c value shows Lichen moth
216 4c value shows Puriri moth

212

213

214

215

216

United States of America

This is another 'life-study'. The group—if one may call it that—will satisfy the most fastidious collector who wishes to concentrate on a single country.

In spite of the fact that almost every collector in the States appears to collect USA, and that many of them specialise to a high degree, the story has not yet been completely told, for discoveries are being made continuously, and a delightful thing about American collectors is that they do not hesitate to publish their findings in the philatelic press, in pamphlets and books.

As with all big countries that have had an early postal service, the point at which to start presents something of a problem. It is not very helpful to say 'start at the beginning', for much of the early material is not easy to find, nor is it cheap. Likewise, to say 'start with this year's issues and move backwards' could mean a long delay before some of the charm of the early material is experienced. A happy medium would be to choose a series, such as that of 1922—32 showing presidents and American scenes, and pick up all the modern commemoratives as they come along; also select a single early stamp, like the Houdon bust of George Washington on the 2 cents (carmine and shades) of 1914—21 (numerals in lower corners). This study could fill 50 or more pages of a loose-leaf album; a bit monotonous to the casual viewer, but a delight for the specialist. What are the 'many splendoured things' of US philately? Confining the subject to the mideighties, the Postmaster's Provisionals should take pride of place. These Provisionals, authorised by Act of Congress of 3 March 1845, first appeared in New York in July 1845, when the Postmaster, Robert H. Morris, issued a 5 cents stamp showing the head of Washington, taken from the current banknotes die.

217 US 'Black Jack' stamp, the 1863 2c black The head is that of Andrew Jackson, who died in 1845

218

219

220

221

222

223

218 George Washington on a US 90c stamp. Washington was President 1789—97
219 John Adams, US President 1797—1801 on the 2c stamp
220 Thomas Jefferson, President 1801—09, on a US 5c stamp
221 Abraham Lincoln, President of the United States 1861—65, on a 16c stamp
222 US $1 stamp showing President Woodrow Wilson, 1913—21
223 President Roosevelt, 1933—45, on a 1c US pictorial stamp

224 Patriotic US cover showing the Confederacy flag and franked with two 10c Jefferson Davis stamps
225 The US fast mail. The official inauguration of the 'railroad post office' was authorised on August 24, 1864, although mail had been carried by rail unofficially as early as 1831

224

Envelopes were also issued by other Postmasters as well as stamps. As these Provisionals come into the world's rarities class, they are not likely to be acquired by the average collector who, if interested, has to make do with some of the reprints that are available.

When the Government issued postage stamps for general issue on 1 July 1847, Provisionals were then unnecessary.

Among these general issues of 1847 onwards there are many individual items and some sets that are within the price range of the average collector. But the prices of many of these earlies are increasing gradually each year, so the collector who is going to make USA a speciality would be well advised to be on the lookout for these items. Cheap specimens that have the designs off-centre are not a good investment—fine as temporary space fillers, but if money is being spent it is far wiser to pay more for well centred copies.

It might not be out of place here to 'tip' one stamp in particular that could catch up in price and popularity with the famous Penny Black of Great Britain, viz, the 'Black Jack' of 1863. This handsome 2 cents showing Andrew Jackson's head, taken from a miniature by J. W. Dodge, makes a very fine speciality—as so many Americans are finding, hence the reason for its increasing catalogue price. Again, well centred copies are the ones to search for.

First day covers have always been popular in America and within recent years many excellent designs on envelopes have been produced for the first day of issue of new stamps. Modern productions are easy to acquire, but it is the 'earlies' from the Colombian Exposition issue of 1893 that require a diligent search before they are run to earth.

Other branches of the American scene include Imperforate Coils, Vending and Affixing Machine Perforations, Booklet Panes, Special Delivery, Registration, Postage Dues and Offices in China.

There are also Occupation stamps and overprints of the Allied Military Governments (US and Britain) for civilian mail in Allied occupied districts (1943–47), Officials, Postal Savings Mail and Savings Stamps, Newspaper and Periodical Issues, Parcel Post, Special Handling, Carriers' stamps, Post Office Seals and Bureau Precancels.

In addition to all these items, each worthy of a specialised study, there are stamped Envelopes and Postal Cards, Revenues, Consular Service Fees, Embossed Revenue Stamped Paper, Private Proprietary stamps, Die, Plate, and Trial Colour Proofs.

Regular stamps overprinted 'Specimen', Postage stamps encased in a circular metal frame for use as money during the Civil War, US Postage Currency, International Reply Coupons

226 The 5c US stamp issued by the postmaster of New York in July 1845. It was recess printed in black

227 Very rare US cover. The 5c Benjamin Franklin stamp of 1847 has blue PAID cancellation

228 A rare block of four US stamps, the Trans-Mississippi Exposition set of 1898. The $1 value is titled 'Western Castle in Storm', but in fact the design is from J. M. McWhirter's painting of Scottish highland cattle 'The Vanguard'

229—241 United Nations stamps are included by many collectors in the modern USA group. They were first issued in 1951, are easy to collect and tell a fine story of the organisation's achievements

242 New York Postmaster's provisionals on a cover of 1845. These stamps are quite rare

243 Wells Fargo and Co cover of 1873 with US imprinted stamp and a Canadian adhesive stamp, and handstamps of New York and London. It was sent from Canada to England

244 Two US moon landing commemorative stamps on a cover posted aboard the USS *Hawkins*

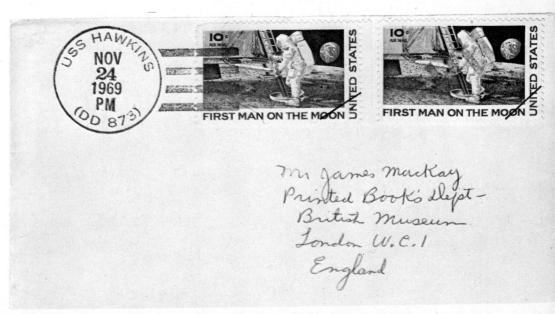

245 Precancel EASTON PA. on US 1968 6c stamp showing Washington
246 Precancel CONCORD, N.H. on US 1932 3c stamp
247 US 1941 6c airmail stamp showing a mail plane
248 3c US stamp of 1955 celebrating the centenary of the Soo Locks

249 1955 3c US stamp marking the 200th anniversary of Fort Ticonderoga

250 Jefferson's home at Monticello is shown on the 1956 20c US stamp
251 The centenary of overland mail in the US is commemorated on this 1958 4c stamp
252 The centenary of the Pony Express is recorded in 1960 on this 4c US stamp

253 The first automated post office at Providence, Rhode Island, was marked by a special US stamp in 1960
254 The first International Postal Conference in Paris in 1863 was commemorated in 1963 by this 15c US air mail stamp. Montgomery Blair, who is shown, was the US Postmaster General who introduced the idea of a universal postal treaty

255 US postcard, with imprinted stamp, of 1880 bearing a cork cancellation

(from 1907), Locals (there are many cheap and crude reprints of these) and Local Hand-stamped covers—all these are of interest.

Telegraph stamps were produced by individual companies and these are popular, as are the National Christmas seals of 1907 to date, issued by the American National Red Cross and the National Tuberculosis Association.

The Confederate States stamps of 1861 form yet another highly specialised branch, but like the Carriers' stamps and the Locals they are inclined to be expensive.

The foregoing will give the collector some idea of the wide scope of US philately.

Further reading

Catalogue of United States Stamps Specialized, published annually by Scott Publishing Co, 604 Fifth Avenue, New York, NY 10020.

United States Postage Stamps. An illustrated descriptive book of all postage and special stamps issued by the Post Office Department since 1847. From Superintendent of Documents, US Government Printing Office, Washington DC 20402, 1972.

Private Die Proprietary Medicine Stamps by G. B. Griffenhager. American Topical Association, 3306 N. 50th Street, Milwaukee, Wis. 53216, 1969.

Postal History of United States Forces in British Solomon Islands Protectorate During World War II by S. C. Jersey. The American Philatelic Society Inc, 1968.

The Harry F. Allen Collection of Black Jacks (a study of the stamp and its use) by Maryette Lane. The American Philatelic Society Inc, 1969.

US Departmental Specimen Stamps by W. V. Combs. The American Philatelic Society Inc, 1965.

Postal History of the United States Virgin Islands by J. Alfred Birch. The American Philatelic Society Inc, 1966.

The Private Local Posts of the United States by D. S. Patton. Robson Lowe Ltd, 50 Pall Mall, London SW1, 1967.

United States 24c Air Mail Inverted Center of 1918 by Henry M. Goodkind. The Collectors Club, New York.

Confederate States of America, Special Postal Routes by Lawrence L. Shenfield. The Collectors Club, New York.

The Pony Express by M. C. Nathan and W. S. Boggs. The Collectors Club, New York.

United States, the 1851–57 Twelve Cent Stamp by Mortimer L. Neinken. The Collectors Club, New York.

Civil War Prisons and their Covers by Earl Antrim. The Collectors Club, New York.

256 Confederate States stamp of 1862 portraying Jefferson Davis. Produced by De la Rue, it is the only American stamp produced outside America

257

258

259

257 One of the most valuable misprints. A block of four 24c US air mail of 1918 with the plane upside down
258 US 5c Lincoln Stamp of 1963
259 US 2c Arbor Day Stamp of 1932

260 The US 3c Charter Oak Connecticut tercentenary stamp
261 US 3c Army issue of 1937

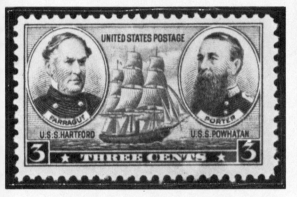

262 US 3c Navy issue of 1937
263 1948 US 3c Lincoln stamp showing part of the Gettysburg address

264 US Civil War Centennial stamp of 1961 showing a sea coast gun
265 US Civil War Centennial Stamp of 1962 showing a rifleman at Shiloh

266 US Civil War Centennial stamp of 1963 showing Blue and Gray at Gettysburg
267 US Civil War Centennial stamp of 1964 showing the Battle of the Wilderness

268 US 5c Davy Crockett stamp of 1967

Refreshment for those on the York–London mail coach
at 'the last change in'. The date is pre-1846.

Thematics and Cinderellas

Stamp collecting began in the 1850s when, perhaps as a change from gluing scraps and greetings cards in an album, some gentlefolk thought that a collection of stamps from different parts of the world could be gathered together and glued in an album under the names of their respective countries. Such an album, though not containing many specimens, would entertain visitors in the drawing room, when conversation showed signs of flagging.

As the Victorian years went on their stately way, the hobby rapidly increased in popularity and began to develop into a serious subject. This would be the time when little Agatha would be severely reprimanded by Papa for threading hundreds of Penny Reds tightly together in order to make a silly snake. (This explains why early British Penny Reds and Penny Lilacs are sometimes found with a pin (needle) hole through the centre).

As more and more countries followed Great Britain's lead in issuing stamps, the collectors would want to know more about their stamps: when they were issued, how many specimens to a series, how many in a sheet, who printed them, the watermarks, what did the design represent—thus the science of philately was born.

Towards the end of the First World War, one of the early themes, or topics, emerged—war stamps. Here was a comparatively new idea in collecting, where a subject common to a number of countries could be built up to illustrate a story.

Into this particular group came overprints, such as WAR TAX with a surcharge, the premium going to a charity. Then the theme was further developed by the addition of postmarks and censored letters from 'the front'; perhaps a postcard showing an artist's impression of a battle, or a simulated Zeppelin raid with the dirigible caught in the stabbing beams of searchlights—all such items helped to build up an interesting and exciting pictorial story.

At the beginning of the century a 'subject' collection was limited mostly to monarchs, presidents and scenes.

There were not many enthusiasts for this type of collecting, but in the 1920s rulers in some nations began to be replaced on postage stamps by objects of a more popular nature. So it became possible for collectors to choose a subject out of a wide range.

Today the choice is so wide that no matter what one's interest—and the tendency is to select a subject that reflects one's trade, profession or leisure occupation—there are stamp designs to illustrate it.

Among the most popular topics are religion, sport, flowers, native costumes and ships, and many countries are 'cashing in' on this type of collecting by producing long sets of colourful pictorials in a wide variety of designs. This can make it something of a problem for the collector to decide on a group, but once having made a choice then the pleasure begins. It will soon be realised that the thrill of the chase is as exciting as that experienced by the more serious approach of the dedicated specialist seeking elusive re-entries on a classical issue.

To illustrate how a theme can be developed from personal inclination, a few words to show how a collection was built up. The writer, having been in journalism since student days, selected a theme that would reflect the chosen occupation: stamps depicting full-time journalists, old and new printing presses, front pages of newspapers, all were garnered and worked into a story 'Gentlemen of the Press!'

It is quite extraordinary how many designs from different countries helped to build up the theme. To illustrate how the story develops out of simple research, here are some of the stamps with brief notes.

Johann Gutenberg was born in 1400 in Mainz, Germany, where, at the age of 44, he set up a small printing works. It was he who invented movable type, which eventually made the production of books a commercial possibility. Gutenberg is shown with his press and a modern rotary machine in the background on a 1948 stamp of Hungary.

In 1952 USA commemorated the 500th Anniversary of the printing of the Holy Bible from movable type by Gutenberg. The vignette shows the printer displaying a proof of the Bible to the Elector of Mainz. Gutenberg also appears on stamps from Bulgaria (1940) and Germany (1939, 1947).

The first Russian printer was Ivan Fedorov; a 1933 stamp from Russia commemorated his death in 1583.

Gaspar Karoli, who translated the Bible into the Hungarian language (1590), is depicted examining his Bible, with the printing press in the background, on a 1934 stamp from Hungary.

Bulgaria commemorated the 500th Anniversary of the invention of machine printing and the centenary of N. Karastojanov with an issue in 1940, one value of which shows the printer.

After early printers early hand-presses can be shown. In 1639 an Englishman, Stephan Daye, took a machine to America and opened a printing shop in Cambridge, Massachuestts, where he produced *The Freeman's Oath*. His machine appears on a 1939 USA stamp commemorating the 300th Anniversary of printing in Colonial America.

In 1943 San Marino brought out a Press Propaganda set, on the low values of which appear a very early press and on the high values front pages of newspapers.

The tercentenary of the introduction of printing

269–272 Four stamps from an Australian set depicting birds:
269 6c blue-faced honeyeater
270 13c red-necked avocet
271 20c golden whistler
272 24c azure kingfisher

273–276 Four stamps from a Hungarian set of flowers— a popular theme in many countries

277 A block of four fauna and flora from Dominica. The 6c shows a giant green turtle, the 24c flying fish, the 38c the anthurium lily, the 60c Imperial and red-necked parrots

BLUE-FACED HONEYEATER

6c

AUSTRALIA

269

RED-NECKED AVOCET

13c

AUSTRALIA

270

GOLDEN WHISTLER

20c

AUSTRALIA

271

AZURE KINGFISHER

24c

AUSTRALIA

272

FELSZABADULÁSUNK 20. ÉVFORDULÓJÁNAK EMLÉKÉRE 1965

50f

MAGYAR POSTA

FELSZABADULÁSUNK 20. ÉVFORDULÓJÁNAK EMLÉKÉRE 1965

2Ft

MAGYAR POSTA

FELSZABADULÁSUNK 20. ÉVFORDULÓJÁNAK EMLÉKÉRE 1965

2.50Ft

MAGYAR POSTA

FELSZABADULÁSUNK 20. ÉVFORDULÓJÁNAK EMLÉKÉRE 1965

3Ft

MAGYAR POSTA

FAUNA FLORA

DOMINICA

GREEN TURTLE

6c

Chelonia mydas

DOMINICA

FLYING FISH Cypselurus heterurus

24c

DOMINICA

ANTHURIUM LILY

Anthurium andraeanum

38c

DOMINICA

IMPERIAL AND RED-NECKED PARROTS

SISSEROU Amazona imperialis JACQUOT Amazona arausiaca

60c

DOMINICA

73

cuttings or drawings. They may add to the story, but they will take away winning points when the judges cast their critical eyes over the entry. The 'stamp's the thing' and should tell the reason for its inclusion with a simple caption. If, for instance, the theme is Railways, it is permissible to show, say, an early rail ticket or an extract from a time-table if they have a direct connection with a particular train or station shown on a stamp, but don't show part of a guard's flag, or the wrapper from a bar of chocolate because it came out of a platform slot machine! (Yes, these exhibits once turned up at a club meeting, the excuse being that the flag was an antique, and the wrapper came from a famous brand that used to sustain hungry travellers! Now the brand of chocolate and the penny machines have disappeared).

One of the competition judges with whom I have worked at exhibitions is Kay Horowicz, a well-known philatelic writer. At a big society competition she was judging she was asked to observe the following rules:

'Exhibits should consist of not more than 16 pages illustrating a theme. The theme may be either purpose of issue or any subject capable of illustration by the designs on the stamps. Marks will not be given for photographs, postcards or cuttings. Neither will they be given for drawings unless these explain the theme. Writing-up should be concise.'

The marks to be obtained were as follows: 1. Knowledge, coverage and development of the theme—50. 2. Writing-up and display—20. 3. Conditions—15. 4. Originality—15.

Competitors should study very thoroughly the rules governing any competition entered. My personal feeling is that a thematic collection gains a lot in public appeal when it contains a few interesting items other than stamps, yet having a close bearing on the subject. But as there are one or two 'governing bodies' that are imposing rules on some international and national exhibitions, it is best for a competitor to be thoroughly conversant with all the conditions to be observed by entrants.

Sources of supply

This is sometimes a problem for the collector concentrating on a particular topic. Unlike the search for general issues of a country, there are not so many dealers in the field of thematics for the simple reason it is in its way specialised, yet specimens do not usually carry the price tag of specialist material. A dealer often has to break into a set in order to extract one item for a customer, and as this can spoil a future sale of that set the dealer is not too happy over such a transaction.

Fortunately there are some traders who cater for the awkward customer requiring special designs. A search through any popular stamp magazine will soon bring about a contact.

281

282

283

284

285

281–285 Five stamps with a fairy tales theme: **281,282** 1966 Luxembourg stamps **283** 1969 Bulgarian stamp **284,285** West German stamps

286–289 Butterflies and moths theme on a selection from a set of Papua and New Guinea. Butterflies are a popular theme in many countries

290

291

292

293

290—297 A printing and press theme:
290 West German Gutenburg Bible stamp
291 Printing press on West German stamp
292 5c Canada stamp celebrating a free press
293 Swedish 1 kr stamp showing a printer and a library
294—297 Four stamps from Holland from a set celebrating printing anniversaries

294

295

296

297

298

299

300

301

302

303

298—303 A sailor theme from Australia:
298 40c Abel Tasman
299 50c William Dampier
300 75c James Cook
301 $1 Matthew Flinders
302 $2 George Bass
303 $4 Phillip Parker King

304—307 Swiss stamps show girls in costumes. Four are illustrated from the years 1935 and 1936

Clubs

Although collecting to a theme or topic has become very popular, out of the vast number of general clubs in existence only a few are devoted exclusively to thematics. Here again, an Editor of a magazine will supply the necessary contacts.

The Year Books published by organisations such as the British Philatelic Association and the American Philatelic Society also carry details of clubs, so there should be no difficulty in finding the right one.

America has the biggest organisation in the world devoted to the subject under review. Known as the American Topical Association, it has published monographs on most of the popular subjects and has done a lot to foster this branch of the hobby in the USA.

The ATA, the initials by which the Association is generally known, also publishes a periodical, *Topical Times*. This gives news, check lists and articles concerning all aspects of the subject. The Secretary of this Association is Karl L. Keldenich, PO Box 1062, Milwaukee, Wisconsin 53201, USA.

Exhibitions

So popular has thematic collecting become that exhibitions devoted entirely to it are developing in many countries, especially America and Britain. The annual British Philatelic Exhibition in London has a strong section devoted to thematics. Here successful competitors can win medals and certificates; a large silver cup and a cash prize is also donated by Link House Publications to encourage collectors to participate.

A thematic exhibition is also run annually by Luton and District Philatelic Society. Details of this exhibition are available from UK Thematics Publicity, 22 Blundell Rd, Luton, Beds.

There are many other international, national and local exhibitions that feature thematics. Advance information of most of them is given in the philatelic press.

Cinderellas

About thirteen years ago a new branch of the hobby began to develop. It started as a small club in London with about eighty members. Today the cult has many thousands of followers in Great Britain and the Americas and is fast finding devotees in Australia, France—in fact in most countries where stamps are collected.

Even the name of the group is romantic—Cinderella Stamp Club, but it is no fairy tale, it is a true story of a vast body of collectors seeking adventure along partly untrodden paths.

But why Cinderella?

Simple: the poor, attractive little sister of Philately—or to be less poetic, the neglected side of the hobby, the once unpopular and sometimes frowned-upon groups such as phantoms, fakes, forgeries, propaganda labels.

So now this former down-trodden member of the family is accepted by nearly all philatelists. The glass slipper of respectability fits, and Cinderella is married to her Prince Philately!

The joy of this type of collecting is that a lot of it is still pioneer work. Discoveries are still being made in each section, some of them rare in as much as only one or two specimens have so far come to light.

At the moment, Cinderella material—with the exception of locals—does not normally achieve high prices; but such is the growing popularity of the various groups that it will not be long before the scarcity of many items is realised and—wham!—up will go the prices. Even now the material appearing in the general auctions is attracting determined bidders.

If Cinderellas are going to be chosen as a side-line, or even the only entry into the world of stamps, it is best for the newcomer to concentrate on one section at first; even then it will soon be realised what is meant by 'pioneer work'.

The main sections are as follows:

Locals: the most important and popular section of all; considered by many philatelists to be an independent group on its own. Locals are issued by authorities, or private concerns, to frank mail within a limited (local) area.

Fiscals: broadly a form of tax or duty stamp (revenue) on receipts etc. Many countries produce special issues for this purpose; those from Mexico, Canada, USA and France, for example, are very attractive. Postage stamps may also be used as receipt stamps: these have little appeal to collectors, but fiscals used for postage are in great demand.

Fakes: these are originally genuine stamps that have been tampered with, such as cutting off perforations to create an imperforate specimen; removal of, or alterations to postmarks; re-gumming and other forms of faking.

Forgeries: imitations of genuine stamps for fraudulent purposes. Postal forgeries of current stamps are made illegally to deceive postal authorities and, in times of war, legally to deceive the enemy. Philatelic forgeries are made to defraud the trade and the collector.

Phantoms: Cinderellas started with these. The term represents stamps issued by fictitious countries, illegal 'governments' or would-be leaders, and some organisations with genuine causes.

Propaganda: labels in this section may be sub-divided into Charity, Exhibitions and Publicity. It is a large group, and it can be further sub-divided into specimens that are intended to look like stamps, and those that are small 'stickers', usually imperforate.

Telegraph: used for the payment of fees on telegrams.

Registration labels: placed on letters and

324 Telegraph stamps of Great Britain, private and Post Office issues, are a highly specialised study. This is a £5 (orange) of the 1876—80 series

325 Harold Waterton (left) and the author (right) looking at the famous Waterton collection of Emergency Strike Post Labels, one of which is shown above

326 An 1880 5 kop of the Zemstvo (Russian local) post of Zemliansk
327 Zenkor 3 kop stamp of 1879—88
328 A 2 kop stamp of Zolotonosha of 1885

326 **327** **328**

329, 330 Two inter-postal seals used between 1864 and 1890 for official purposes in Egypt. One is from Alexandria and the other from Wadi-Haifa

334

333 The Court Bureau ran a private letter-collecting service on Sundays from 1889 to 1891. The 1d red stamp was issued in 1890.
334 The German town of Bamberg operated a local post between 1896 and 1900. This is a 2pf Bamberg stamp

331

333

331 An advertisement for the Coolgardie Cycle Express Co organised in 1893 by James A. Healy to carry mail and gold dust during the Western Australia gold rush
332 A bicycle post ran between Fresno and San Francisco during a railway strike in 1894. It was run by Arthur Banta who issued this stamp

332

335

336

337

338

339

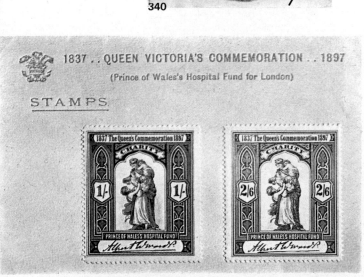

340

335–340 Zemstvo stamps. Zemstvo posts were local Russian posts which operated between 1865 and the First World War. Thousands of designs were issued

335 Key-type printed stamp of Ardatov
335 Zenkov issue, the design being copied from a Danish stamp
337 Key-type stamp of Bakhmut
338 A Duitrof stamp cancelled by pen
339 Typeset stamp of Bielozersk
340 Negative seal cancellation on a stamp of Vessiegonsk

341

342

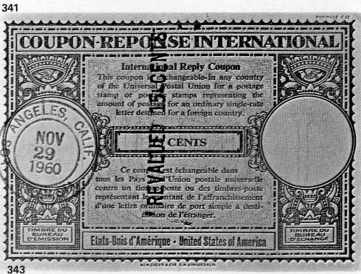

343

341 Hospital charity labels, produced at the time of Queen Victoria's Jubilee in 1897, on a souvenir envelope
342 1972 Christmas seal. Christmas seals decorate envelopes used at Christmas time and are usually sold by organisations collecting for charity

343 An international reply coupon from Los Angeles, California, bearing a surcharge increasing the value from 13c to 15c. International reply coupons are usable at all post offices and are used to send foreign correspondents the return postage

parcels that require special care to ensure safe delivery.

Strike Post: a new group; created when postal workers 'down tools' because they want their wages to go up.

Canada had a postal strike in March 1970 when a label was issued; but the strike with the biggest distruption to services, and which produced the greatest amount of philatelic material, occured in 1971 in Great Britain, from 20 January to 7 March. The Minister of Posts, realising the postal service to the nation had broken down completely, allowed private posts to operate. Armed with an authority from a postmaster to conduct a private postal delivery service, a great many firms and individuals decided to institute such a service and to issue labels with which to frank mail.

Many weird and wonderful labels were produced by over 250 private services. Obviously with the once jealously guarded monopoly of the Post Office temporarily waived, certain firms and individuals with an eye on the philatelic market had a bonanza. However, many operated a genuine, useful service and if some of the stamps issued were unnecessary, they added novelty and a little light relief during a frustrating strike.

These labels are best collected on cover, for this gives some evidence of a legitimate private postal service.

Further reading

Books on some of the groups mentioned in this chapter are not always easy to obtain from stamp dealers. The best plan is to consult the lists of firms specialising in philatelic literature. Again a magazine can supply titles of some books published and addresses of suppliers of literature.

Here is a short guide to a few important works on some of the subjects.

Phantom Philately, by F. J. Melville. The Philatelic Institute. (No longer in business).

Cinderella Stamps, by L. N. and M. Williams. William Heinemann Ltd, London, 1970.

Catalogue of British Local Stamps, by Gerald Rosen. The BLSC Publishing Co, London N1, 1970.

Literature of Cinderella Philately, by H. E. Tester. The Cinderella Stamp Club, 1972. *From:* E. W. Stannard, 26 Somerset Road, Harrow, HA1 4NG.

'Strike Posts'—an extensive, illustrated listing, *Stamp Year Book 1972* (Link House Publications).

344 The Electric Telegraph Company director's message stamp of 1855. Four directors had the privilege indicated

345 A specimen sheet of a proposed set of stamps for Sealand. They were never officially recognized

347

346, 347 The Great Britain Silver Jubilee ½d stamp of 1935 and a propaganda stamp of 1944 based upon it

National Savings stamps 1916 to 1960

1916   1918   1940   1940   1941

1942   1944

1949   1953   1953   1954   1954

1951   1958   1958   1960   1960

349

ROBERT BURNS 4d

1759 – 1796

348 A Cinderella label from Scotland that should *not* have paid the postage on a letter, but did!
349 Great Britain National Savings stamps of 1916 to 1960

351

350 Early stamp for St. John's College, Oxford
351 Special private stamps produced for use on mail from ships blockaded in the Suez canal, 1968

This is a combined branch of the hobby that in recent years has climbed high in the philatelic popularity charts.

One of the reasons for this is that the old is linked with the new, the rare with the inexpensive. Couple this to the fact that many historical events have been commemorated with a pictorial envelope, the revival of picture postcard and postal stationery collecting and the acceptance by all collectors of the increasing value of postal history as the solid foundation upon which philately is built, and it will be realised why this branch is now so popular.

First a few notes on the Envelope. Before 1840 and the Uniform Penny Postage scheme of Rowland Hill, users of the postal service were careful not to enclose their letters in any form of covering, such as a wrapper or an envelope; to do so would have resulted in double postage being charged. A single sheet, folded two or three times and sealed with wax or a small circular wafer, was the recognised method of preparing a letter for posting.

The majority of these early letters were addressed to solicitors or tradesmen and the messages usually brief and to the point. When the missive was to a friend or relative, the sender sometimes overcame the single sheet restriction by employing criss-cross writing, that is writing in the normal horizontal manner and then continuing the letter by writing from the bottom to the top of the sheet. So that the vertical writing did not obscure the horizontal lines, a thin quill or nib was used. Occasionally one of these early criss-cross letters is found in which the writer, with a great deal of news to impart, has also written diagonally, from corner to corner! Difficult to read? Well, our ancestors had plenty of leisure time to attend to their correspondence!

On 1 May 1840 Great Britain issued the world's first adhesive postage stamp; it was valid for use by the public on 6 May. At the same time a pictorial envelope and a letter-sheet were issued, in each case a one penny in black and a two pence in blue. The design by a Royal Academician, William Mulready, attempted to show the people the far-reaching benefits of the new Uniform Penny Postage. But the fickle public, even in those patriotic Victorian days, treated the whole thing as a joke and ridiculed the pictorial 'Mulready' out of existence. Disappointed at the public's reaction, the GPO eventually withdrew the innovation.

Facsimilies, forgeries, caricatures and comic envelopes quickly followed, and today these are highly prized items.

Among the more sensible pictorial envelopes produced was the series of ten designs by Fores of Piccadilly, London. These were by the young Doyle brothers, who were talented artists, and the designs portrayed Courting, Music, Dancing, Hunting, Racing, Coaching, Shooting, Civil, Military and Christmas. The latter, drawn by Richard Doyle, was the first Christmas pictorial envelope in the world and is very scarce, especially since both postal historians and Christmas card collectors are always searching for specimens.

Another item that is popular with cover collectors is the South Kensington envelope of 2 July 1890, issued for the Post Office Penny Postage Jubilee. This attractive commemorative printed in blue has a pictorial correspondence card inside showing the likeness of Rowland Hill and underneath HE GAVE US PENNY POSTAGE. As was usual in Victorian days, when cartoonists seized upon every opportunity to ridicule political and civic affairs, the envelope and its card was lampooned by cartoonist Harry Furniss. The original envelope and card are inexpensive today, but with the enthusiasm for these items increasing rapidly, anyone interested in such things should buy now.

The early pictorial envelopes are a fascinating study, but some expert guidance is necessary before hunting for them. Volume 1 of *The Encyclopaedia of British Empire Postage Stamps*, published by Robson Lowe Ltd, has a large section devoted to the Mulready envelope, comic envelopes, propaganda envelopes, commemorative envelopes and letter sheets. This is now a scarce volume.

The Mulready Envelope and its Caricatures by Major E. B. Evans was a famous book first published in 1891. It has been republished by S. R. Publishers Ltd, East Ardsley, Wakefield.

The Victorian material just mentioned makes a fine beginning to any collection of Covers, and there are of course other early groups that are big studies in themselves, such as the American Civil War patriotic envelopes, and many other less dramatic events recorded in pictorial form on an envelope; but much of this material is now becoming quite expensive.

It is when the collection takes in modern covers that a vast, inexpensive field is opened up. Thanks to the ingenuity of Post Offices of many nations, to organisations and a few active dealers, many historic and social events, past and present, are being recorded in the form of First Day Covers—popularly known by the abbreviation FDC.

A first day cover is an envelope bearing a new issue of a stamp or stamps, postmarked on the day of issue.

The world's earliest first day cover is a Great Britain Penny Black on cover postmarked on the day it was issued—6 May 1840—and obviously rare. The Victorians had no idea they were making philatelic history in those far-off days, and they would have been not a little

352 The Guildhall, London, Jubilee postcard of 1890
353 The South Kensington Jubilee correspondence card, 1890
354 The envelope for the South Kensington Jubilee card, 1890

355 A scarce anti-slavery pictorial envelope by J. Valentine

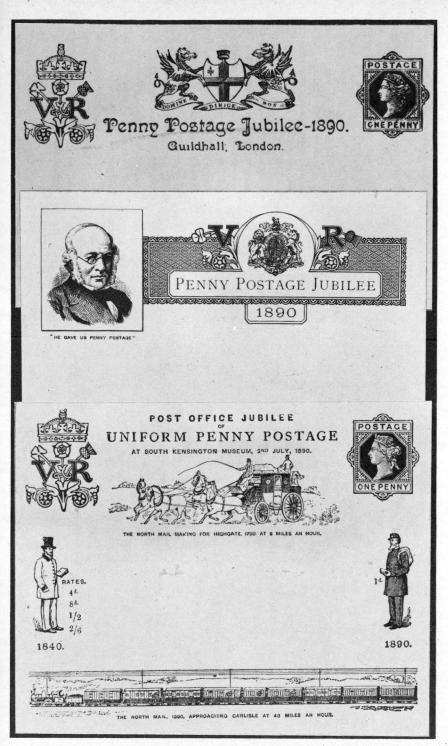

surprised to learn that one of those early covers would one day be worth a small fortune.

First day covers of all the early issues are very desirable items, for they disappear into collections almost as soon as they appear on the market.

Modern FDCs are quite a different matter; unlike their early counterparts they are created especially for the collector. They showed signs of becoming popular about 40 years ago, when certain private firms produced them, first for new issues of stamps, then to commemorate national or local events. The designs on the envelopes, usually on the left half, were often well drawn and when most of these productions went over to multicolour printing the effect was usually pleasing. Little wonder, then, that the modern pictorial envelope or FDC has become so popular.

There are other reasons for this popularity; the design on the envelope, when related to the stamp, can set off an album page very well and obviate additional writing-up. Again, the postmark, often pictorial, adds to the story, so that on one envelope the reasons for an issue or event are illustrated in a compact manner.

In view of the vastness of the group, it is advisable at first to concentrate on a particular theme or country. The choice is extensive: quite a wide section of American political and social history is shown in an expanding series of finely produced pictorial envelopes. The dealers handling these advertise in the American philatelic press; big stores often carry an imposing stock.

There is a delightful series showing the Kings and Queens of England in full colour to match the similar theme on a long set of stamps from Barbuda. The Royal Air Force are represented by a long series, with profits from their sale going to a benevolent fund, while the National Army Museum sets show uniforms of many early regiments in their brilliant colours.

New Zealand is another fruitful source of material; their Health Camps series being particularly attractive.

Both Czechoslovakia and Hungary also produce official FDCs for their new issues, the former often employing famous national artists to create the designs.

Spain produce some real works of art to match their commemorative sets, such as the Galvez series for the attractive Costumes and Provinces sets.

There are three sections of the philatelic community buying these special covers regularly: the collector of a particular country, the subject collector and, of course, the covers enthusiast. That is why it is wise to acquire new covers while they are still readily available. As an instance—Israel. When this ancient country regained independence in 1948, the first issue

Mrs Powell
Quex Park
Nr Margate
Kent

POSTAGE TWO PENCE.

W. MULREADY. R.A.   JOHN THOMPSON.

Thos. Jerrom Esq.
Secretary to the Bombay
Auxiliary Bible Society
The Esplanade
Bombay.

356 A Mulready envelope posted in London, bearing the special inner London area Maltese Cross cancellation, which has a small cross at the top and a numeral in the centre
357 Mauritius 1d 'Post Office' stamps of 1897. This cover was sold for a record $380,000 (£160,000) at Harmers in 1968

358 A postcard produced in Canada in 1898 at the time of the Boer War

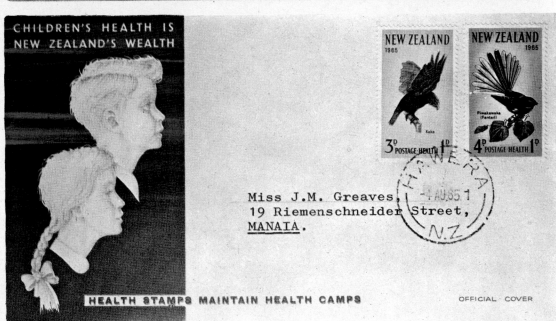

359 A first day cover showing New Zealand Health stamps of 1965

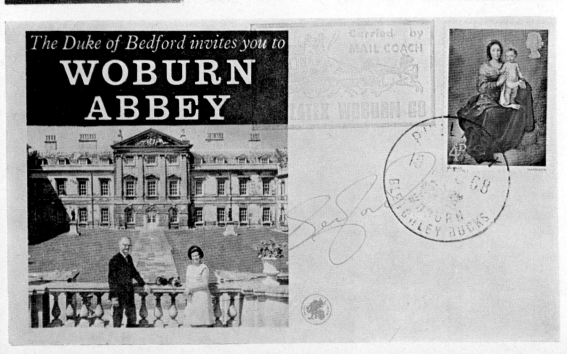

360 A British cachet mark advertising a special mail coach delivery from Woburn in 1968

361 Discovered in Scotland, this letter bears ten Penny Blacks—the largest number ever found on a first day cover

362 Cards with designs in woven coloured silks were produced in England for use with commemorative stamps of 1968—70

363 This cover left Plymouth, England, in August 1966 and was posted back from Sydney, Australia c/o *Gipsy Moth IV*, on which Sir Francis Chichester was making his historic single-handed round-the-world trip. Back at Plymouth it received the special 'Welcome' postmark

364 British Army philatelists in the Far East Land Forces, service their own special Christmas covers. Profits from sales go to charity.

361

1620 · Mayflower · 1970

362

POSTED AT SEA

AUGUST 1966 - APRIL 1967

On board "Gipsy Moth IV"

PLYMOUTH — SYDNEY — PLYMOUTH

363

364

of stamps of 16 May 1948 showed early coins. Known as the First Coins 'Doar Ivri' set, the stamps have perforated descriptive tabs on the base. Anyone wise enough to forsee the significance of this first issue and who acquired this and the following issues will be feeling very happy, for some of the stamps are now rarities.

With the 1948 set and onwards, attractive FDCs were produced; some of these are very scarce indeed.

The Post Office of Great Britain now sell FDCs with every new issue of stamps. Some of them are quite dull in colour and uninspiring in design, but there have been attractive ones, especially at Christmas time. If the official FDCs are sometimes uninspiring, private enterprise offers an alternative, some of them very pictorial.

Today a first day of issue postmark has little significance as proof of a stamp's first use for postal duty, but pictorial first day covers themselves are no longer a craze but a serious branch of the hobby.

How does one mount this type of material for personal appreciation and display purposes? Stacking them away in a shoe box is not an inspiring method—alright for temporary storage but not very good for enjoyment.

There are albums with transparent pockets, which allow a view of both sides of the cover: single pockets like a book, or two to a page like a stamp album. The latter is more economical—particularly for display purposes. As it is not usually necessary to show both sides of an FDC, four covers paired back to back can be shown per page with the larger albums.

A cheaper method of displaying is to use ordinary album pages (white or black) and mount the covers by means of transparent photographic 'corners'. This is one of the recognised methods for exhibitions purposes.

Further reading

Great Britain First Day Catalogue: Cameo Stamps Ltd, 84 Strand, London WC2, 1970.

Catalogue of Israel: Michael Bale, Ilfracombe, Devon, 1972.

Cover Collecting: James Mackay, Philatelic Publishers Ltd.

Postal stationery

In the very early days of stamp collecting it was quite an achievement for anyone to gather together more than one hundred postage stamps of the world.

To make a collection interesting enough to compete with, say, an album of family photographs or one of crests cut from note-paper and the flaps of envelopes, it was necessary to augment the postage stamp collection by adding revenues from receipts, embossed stamps from legal documents, and impressed

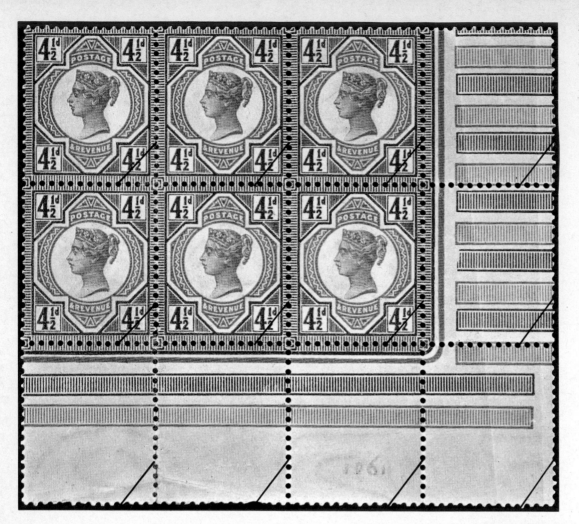

365 Block of six British stamps of the so-called Jubilee series of 1887. The coloured rule round the margin is known as the Jubilee line as it was first used with this series

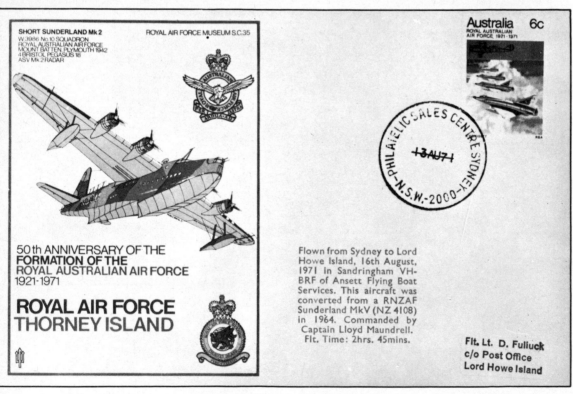

366 A cover from the Royal Air Force Museum series of 1971

367 This Hungarian stamp commemorates the 100th anniversary of the first Hungarian postcard of 1869

368 A postcard showing World Cup Willie, mascot of the World Cup Championships held in Great Britain in 1966. It is franked with a stamp designed for the World Cup and inscribed 'England Winners'. It was posted at Wembley, where the final was held, on the day of issue

369 A printed postcard posted aboard the steamer *Jerusalem* in 1954, showing the postmark used on the ship

stamps cut from envelopes, wrappers or postcards.

Many of the larger stamp albums published in England and Germany in the 19th Century contained illustrated spaces for the complete piece. The early dealers carried postal stationery in their stocks and so built up their trade of philatelic merchandise. It was not a simple matter for them to get stocks of new issues of stamps and stationery in those days; they often had to write out for supplies to the postmaster, or a trader, in the different countries.

In those pioneer days collectors searched for all items of postcards, envelopes, letter cards, wrappers and reply paid cards; many of these were by no means dull in appearance, in fact part of their charm is in their pictorial aspect, especially those from some foreign countries.

Postcards and letter cards lent themselves to the gentle art of decorative appeal, contained in the restricted area of a border on the left half of a card. The term 'charm', as applied to this material, sometimes means overcrowded symbolism or art nouveau, but compared to some of the atrocities that pass as stamp designs today, art of the mid-19th and early 20th centuries is not so heavy and unattractive as some 'moderns' claim it to be.

In 1897 Stanley Gibbons Ltd of London published the eleventh edition of *Priced Catalogue of Envelopes and Wrappers, Post Cards and Letter Cards*. It had 280 illustrated pages, and it covered the issues of the whole world—and sold for one shilling!

The catalogue was quite detailed and did much to put this important section of collecting on a proper footing.

Postal stationery was in vogue for a number of years and then in the reign of King George V it began to lose favour rapidly. The reason was, of course, that collectors and dealers were finding it difficult—and expensive—to keep up to date with all the new stamps being issued. Dealers therefore got rid of most of their stocks of stationery, less was written about it; thus discouraged, collectors generally lost interest in the subject.

For years stationery remained in the doldrums and only specialists were interested in certain items of their own particular country. Now all at once it has started to bounce back into favour. There are many good reasons for this: 1) the interest in modern philatelic cards and covers; 2) the big revival in early picture postcard collecting; 3) the search for all material with a postal history connection; 4) the publication of specialised stamp catalogues with lists of stationery; 5) the manufacture of special albums for cards and envelopes; 6) the publication of comprehensive books on postal stationery in recent years.

Collectors should be indebted to the Americans for the manner in which they have always had faith in this branch of the hobby. While British catalogue publishers and dealers just didn't want to know, the Scott Publishing Company not only continued to print comprehensive listing of entires in their United States *Specialised Catalogues*, but in their *Standard Postage Stamp Catalogue* they listed under the USA section cutouts of stamped envelopes and wrappers, air post stamped envelopes and air letter sheets.

A short chronological list of postal stationery forerunners is as follows:

1608–1797 Venice. Cover at 4 sols showing a coat of arms design.

1653 Paris. 1 sou sheet, for a local post organised by Jean Jacques Renouard de Velager on the authority of Louis XIV. Design showed the coat of arms of M. de Velager.

1790 Luxembourg. Sheets of twenty-five centime tax stamp.

1818 Sardinia. 15, 25 and 50 centesimi sheet. Design: postboy on horseback blowing a horn.

1838 New South Wales. Local embossed one penny letter covers. Design: Royal arms seal of the colony.

1840 Great Britain. Mulready envelopes and letter sheets.

1841 Great Britain. Embossed envelopes.

1853 United States of America. Envelope. George Washington.

1869 Austria. Postcard. Emperor Franz Joseph.

1869 Hungary. Postcard. Emperor Franz Joseph.

1870 Great Britain. Postcard and newspaper wrapper. Victoria.

1873 United States of America. Postcards. Liberty.

1878 Great Britain. Registration envelope.

1892 Great Britain. Letter cards.

1929 United States of America. Air Post envelopes.

1941 Great Britain. Air letter sheets.

As far as the British collector is concerned, postal stationery available to the general public began with the William Mulready envelope (1d black, 2d blue) and the companion letter sheets (1d black, 2d blue).

In January 1841 the envelope with the 1d stamp embossed in pink appeared. A glance at the catalogues will show that this can be quite a detailed study.

Two special events in Victorian cards are the Penny Postage Jubilee (2 July 1890), when a pictorial envelope with an impressed 1d stamp (and a pictorial correspondence card inside) was produced, and the Guildhall Postal Jubilee (16 May 1890) when a 1d carmine card appeared.

In the King George V group items that are worth searching for are: the envelope issued for the British Empire Exhibition at Wembley

370 The first British postcard of 1870

371 Great Britain Christmas air letter of 1971

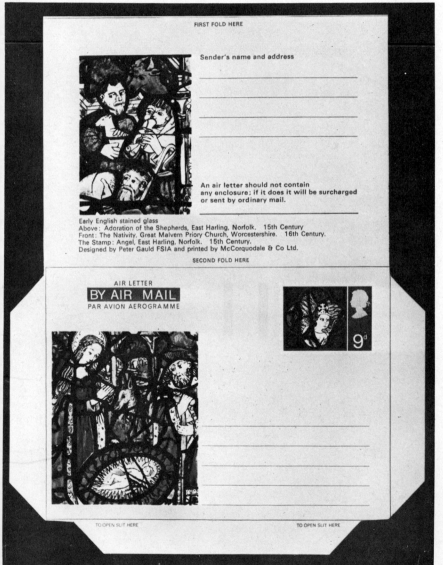

on 23 April 1924 (this cost 1½d; today it is listed at £2 mint or used); and in the following year the same envelope was reissued inscribed 1925. These are listed at £2.50 mint, £5 used. Postcards were also issued for the Exhibition for 1924 and 1925, Inland cards at 1d, and Foreign cards at 1½d. For these 1d and 1½d cards dealers are now asking from £1 to £4 for good examples, with the 1½d Foreign used listed at £10 (1924) and £12.50 (1925).

Yes! adventure may be found by taking up the pursuit of early—and not so early—postal stationery. Rare items are still awaiting to be discovered in bundles of cards, which often show up in dealers' shops or stands at exhibitions and in auction lots. But perhaps enough has been said to set an enthusiast on the trail of what could be a thrilling search for forgotten bygones.

A few words on mounting specimens might be helpful to newcomers to this group.

In the early days special fixed leaf albums were produced by a famous old dealer of London, William Lincoln. He realised that, 'If postcards are put into a stamp album, they are liable, owing to their thickness, to cause the album to break at the binding,' So Mr Lincoln produced a book that made provision for the thickness of the cards by adding extra guards. Cards were mounted by means of hinges at the top or the four corners.

Today the style adapted is to use loose leaf albums of stout paper or card and mount specimens by means of transparent photographic 'corners' in all four corners of the specimen if extra large or heavy, or merely two photographic corners at diagonally opposite corners for small or thin specimens.

Special albums are now issued for cards and covers of all sizes, as has been explained elsewhere in this book.

Reference books

Priced Catalogue of Envelopes and Wrappers, Postcards and Letter Cards. Stanley Gibbons Ltd, 11th edition, 1897.

British Postal Stationery. A priced handbook of the postal stationery of Great Britain by A. K. Huggins. The Great Britain Philatelic Society, London, 1970.

Cancels

When the Post Office was established under an Act of Parliament in 1660, after the Restoration, Colonel Henry Bishop became the lessee. In answer to charges brought against him that mail was being delayed in the post, Bishop, as Master of the Posts, denied the accusations by saying, 'A stamp is invented that is putt upon every letter shewing the day of the moneth that every letter comes to the office, so that no Letter Carryer may dare to detayne a letter from post to post, which before was usual.'

372 A modern interpretation of a very early postmark, used on mail posted from an Essex exhibition in 1969
373 A local British New Guinea postcard with the B.N.G. cancel

374 The 'honour' envelope used by British forces. Not censored at the unit, it could be censored at base. Users certified on their honour that only private matters were included

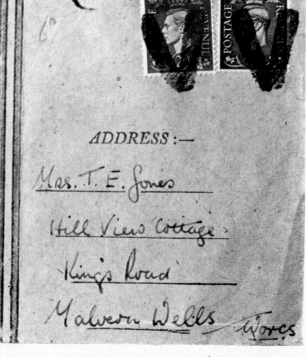

The mark was simplicity itself: a small circle divided by a horizontal line, above which were initials for the month and below figures for the date; thus 'M A' over '22' would mean 22 March.

'Bishop Marks', as they are called, were used on mail in the following cities of England, Ireland, Scotland, and certain of the British colonies, on the dates shown.

London 1661	Philadelphia 1767
Dublin 1672	Boston 1769
Edinburgh 1693	Albany 1774
Exeter 1698	Charlestown 1774
Bristol 1705	Quebec 1776
New York 1758	Calcutta 1776

Another famous—and valuable—mark is that used by William Dockwra (1680) a merchant of the City who organised a local Penny Post for London and surburbs in 1680. The Crown objected to this Penny Post on the grounds that it infringed their monopoly, so it was suppressed two years after its inception.

The postmark used at a Dockwra sorting office was a double-lined triangle with a significant initial in the centre. There were seven sorting offices for London and suburbs and the initials in the centre of the stamps indicated the district, thus 'W' for 'Westminister'.

Mail going through London in early times received a date stamp, but—until 1794—no indication as to whether sorting was done in the morning or the evening. In December 1794 a sorter by the name of Farmer was charged at the Old Bailey with the theft of a letter. At the trial it was questioned whether it could be proved by the postmarking who stamped a letter and which duty shift—morning or evening—was responsible. But although it had to be admitted that both morning and evening cancelling was done with the same handstamp, the man accused of stealing the letter was found guilty and promptly hanged at Tyburn. However, following the trial, a change was made in the postmark design: in February 1795 a single rim was used for morning and a double rim for evening sorting. Unfortunately, poor Farmer was not able to appreciate the subtle change in postmarking that his indiscretion had brought about.

All early cancellation marks have a story to tell, perhaps not as dramatic as Farmer's, but each one of value in showing the development of the postal systems for the despatch and receipt of mail throughout the world.

Like all branches of philately the subject is an immense one, so all-embracing in fact that the enthusiast has to select a limited number of sections for specialising if it is hoped to achieve success.

It is advisable to select for study the postmarks of one country, and having made a choice to sub-divide the particular country into periods

375 A selection of the pictorial postmarks widely used in France

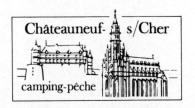

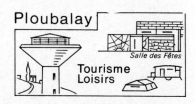

or types of cancellations.

At the turn of the century the old-established family magazine *Bazaar, Exchange and Mart* ran a series of articles on the various marks that had been applied to letters before the introduction of Uniform Penny Postage in 1840. This was written by John Hendy, Curator of the Records Room at the General Post Office, and in 1905 it was published in book form by L. Upcott Gill of London and Charles Scribner and Sons of New York under the title *The History of the Early Postmarks of the British Isles*.

Hendy planned his research in this manner—a good example of how the complicated early markings may be arranged by a student:

London Chief Office
Paid Letters
Sunday Stamps
The Returned Letter Office
Franks or Free Stamps
The Foreign Post Office
Ship Letters
London Receivers—Penny and Twopenny Posts
Country Postmasters
Paid Letters
Penny Posts
Convention or 'Fifth-clause' Posts (village posts, 1801).
Soldiers' and Sailors Cheap Postage Privilege
Scotland
Ireland
Postage Rates

In the Scottish group the famous '131' in the centre of 'rays' is a much sought after cancellation of Edinburgh, and when the even more famous Maltese Cross cancellations are collected the many varieties can be identified by means of published charts. Maltese Crosses to search for are those from London, the Provincial ones of England, Wales and the Channel Islands; Scotland, Ireland, also those in various colours. Since the 'MC' as it is sometimes called, was the cancellation used on the world's first postage stamps, it has attracted a lot of attention from specialists. It can still be bought at a low price 'tying' an imperforate Penny Red of 1841 to the cover. Many of these are clear strikes and easy to identify. Our advice to any interested collector is to buy as many of these entires as possible, for study *and* an appreciation in market value.

When the stamped postcards were introduced by Act of Parliament on 1 October 1871, the cancellations used were the same as those for letters. But to meet the flood of cards posted a new method of defacing them was sought.

Cancelling by perforating was suggested, and a machine was invented by a Mr Sloper. The device pierced the card with small holes in the shape of an arrow.

London and Liverpool tried out Sloper's patent, but it was discontinued in 1875. Postcards with this arrow puncture are certainly worth searching for.

Other fields for collecting are the special cancellations for newspapers, circulars and printed matter, Too Late and Late Fee, registered post, express delivery, parcel post, postage due markings, Undelivered, Delayed, Damaged Mail, 'Posted in Advance for Delivery on Christmas Day' (this is a rare postmark worth finding, particularly the large 'X' in a circle with the name of the town above and 'MAS' below and the date, eg. 19—09 on either side of the 'X').

Royal household, Government departments, Official Paid are yet a few more postal markings that can be built up into separate units. By reading some of the books that round off this chapter, the collector will get further useful ideas.

When we come to the war scene, another vast field is opened. Postmarks and censor marks can trace many of the big campaigns and large concentrations of troops: the Crimean and Boer Wars, World Wars I and II, Korea and Viet-Nam—all are reflected in postal markings. In addition to the Army markings, there is an abundance of early and modern material for the Navy and the Air Force, including mail salvaged from wrecked ships and aeroplanes. Turning to more peaceful events, a magnificent collection may be made from the pictorial cancellations connected with large exhibitions, also sports meetings, including the famous Olympics.

Postal slogans is yet another section worthy of specialised attention. Such slogans go right back to the year 1661, when mail passing through Kent received a slogan 'The Post For All Kent Goes Every Night From The Round House In Love Lane & Comes Every Mor (ning)'.

Many, many years were to pass before slogans were adopted as a serious means of conveying a message not connected with postal matters. In December 1917 Britain in the grip of war introduced machine franked slogans with the patriotic appeal 'BUY NATIONAL WAR BONDS'. Today our daily mail bears advice on countless subjects—where to spend the holidays, exhibitions to visit, famous places and people to remember—all in slogans, often accompanied by a little drawing. So extensive has this subject become that it is possible to separate slogans into hundreds of categories and, if so desired, treat them in a thematic way—such as slogans with a musical connection, or ones commemorating famous people or places, and so on.

As to housing and identifying a collection, the author prefers to collect postmarks on complete covers, but this has the disadvantage, where modern cancellations are concerned, of becoming too bulky if mounted on sheets, and rather 'lost' if merely alphabetically arranged in boxes.

The well-known collector and writer, R. K. Forster, uses a card index system. The postmarks are cut to 4" × 2" and hinged to white filing cards 5" × 3". Notes recording their origin are neatly written or typed on the card. A box or shallow drawer is used to house the collection.

Another method to use is a loose-leaf album page, with the cut-out postmarks mounted in rows and suitably annotated.

Anyone taking up the subject of postmarks, both old and new, is advised to read one or more of the books listed below. If it is felt that the early postmarks are going to be difficult to find or too expensive to buy, then it is best to pass on to the modern material—much of which can be obtained at little or no cost.

Further reading

British Postmarks, A Short History and Guide, by Alcock and Holland. R. C. Alcock Ltd, Cheltenham, 1960.

The Postal Cancellations of London 1840–1890, by H. C. Westley. H. F. Johnson, 44 Fleet Street, London EC4, 1950.

Maltese Cross Cancellations, by Alcock and Holland. R. C. Alcock Ltd, Cheltenham.

Dated Circle Postmarks of Scotland. The Scottish Postmark Society, Edinburgh, 1962.

Scots Local Concellations by C. W. Meredith. R. C. Alcock Ltd, Cheltenham.

Posted in Advance for Delivery on Christmas Day by C. W. Meredith. R. C. Alcock Ltd, Cheltenham.

Postmark Collecting by R. K. Forster. Stanley Paul, London, 1960.

The Skeleton Postmarks of Great Britain by George F. Crabb. British Postmark Society, 1960.

Special Event Postmarks of the United Kingdom by George R. Pearson, London, 1963.

Slogan Postmarks of the United Kingdom by Parsons, Peachey and Pearson, Aylesbury, 1970.

Wembley and Olympic Issues by W. G. Stitt Dibden. The Postal History Society and the GB Philatelic Society, London.

Late Fee and Too Late Stamps by W. G. Stitt Dibden. The GB Philatelic Society, London, 1966.

Isle of Man Postmarks by A. J. P. Massey. Manx Philatelic Society, Isle of Man, 1969.

376 Postmarks of the 16th Olympic Games held in Australia in 1956
377 Field Post Office and censor mark on a special Services envelope—Army Form C.398

From a series of Fore's Coaching Recollections. The
London—Louth mail coach in 1843, changing horses

Within recent years postal history has emerged as a serious, but friendly rival to straightforward stamp collecting.

At one time it was the hobby of a few dedicated philatelists, who methodically studied the subject, occasionally wrote about it in the more learned journals, and quietly searched the dealers, junk shops, bazaars and market stalls for material, for which they often paid but a small price.

A number of factors have contributed to the growth in popularity of the subject: the challenge of pioneer work; the pleasure in the tracking down of obscure items, and the annoyance of many collectors with certain countries for flooding the market with long sets of 'Old Masters' paintings, nudes and novelty printing processes—all masquerading as postage stamps.

Postal history is the study of the origin of the posts, the equipment used in the running of the services, the printed notices, the postal routes, the markings on covers (entires) or packets—the subject is so vast, the avenues for research so numerous that the story has no ending. What is commonplace and perhaps passed by today, will be the postal history of tomorrow.

While few collectors are fortunate enough to get hold of an original clay tablet, incised with a message that had a dramatic meaning a few thousand years ago, notices, documents and letters of a bygone age are still turning up in unexpected places. The 'sources of supply' are many: from the dignified antiquarian bookshop to the interesting market stall; from the high-class auction rooms to the shoe-box of 'odds and ends' on a dusty counter of a stamp dealer in a back street—all these are hunting grounds for the postal historian.

Although so many collectors are now on the look-out for material (and most dealers are well aware what they are looking for!) lucky finds are frequently made. Here are but three instances of the author's personal 'discoveries'. In the window of a London theatrical shop, specialising in ballet and tap shoes, there was a montage of envelopes that had been posted from all parts of the world. Above this was a large card that informed the window-gazer 'From all over the globe our customers write to praise our shoes.' Partly concealed behind an envelope from America was one on which appeared the words 'QUETTA EARTH QUAKE POSTAGE FREE'. I went inside the shop and asked the owner if any of the envelopes were for sale, for I was a stamp collector. 'You can have any five for a dollar' was the reply. I picked out the one from Quetta and held it up. The owner was amused. 'Well to start with, that's got no stamps on it—and you a collector! Well, you can have it for nothing!'

I explained the reason for the absence of stamps and offered 'a dollar' for it, which he accepted—just to please me. This cover is a very scarce item today.

Lucky find number two was at a church jumble sale. On the bric-a-brac stall, smothered by a collection of old pens, pencils, pipes and cheap ash trays was a small box in Tunbridge ware, with Queen Victoria's head on the lid picked out in red to look like a penny postage stamp. I held up the little box. 'How much?' 'Will two shillings be too much?' enquired the lady behind the stall.

Today these Victorian stamp boxes are worth about £3. (I appeased my conscience at the time by being a bit more generous when the church collecting plate came round the Sunday following this lucky purchase!).

The third 'find' was made in a second-hand bookshop near Fleet Street. In the window, for all to see, was a frame in which reposed an old Christmas card with a ticket reading 'The world's first Christmas card, designed by J. C. Horsley for Sir Henry Cole.' With it was the De La Rue reproduction of the card. The price tag showed £5. This was particularly interesting to a philatelist since Sir Henry Cole had been a great postal reformer and advisor to Sir Rowland Hill.

I passed that window everyday for a fortnight on the way to Fleet Street, then eventually succumbed and hesitatingly bought the frame and its contents. Today the Cole-Horsley card is valued at over £150.

Perhaps these instances of lucky finds are not very dramatic, but they do prove that discoveries can be made in unexpected places and that valuable items are not always hidden away. These three finds had been seen by a lot of people, yet no one had realised their value. There is, of course, a 'moral' to this: read up all you can about your hobby.

An interesting trend today is to specialise in the postal history of one's own town. A number of collectors have done this and have recorded their findings in monographs.

The big towns are not always the most interesting for the student, since many have been written up already, and unless one can delve more deeply into the history of a place, originality of approach is difficult.

With a small town, county or zone, the prospects are quite exciting; but before taking up research work it is best to find out through the local library and the philatelic society if anyone else has worked on the subject. If no one has researched it, then the field is clear.

Before embarking on the work, three attributes are essential: enthusiasm, patience and plenty of spare time.

The first task is to seek an interview with the head postmaster and explain the project. He

378 A Free Frank signed by Charles, Fifth Duke of Richmond, Postmaster General

379 An official notice to all postmasters dated 7 May 1840 enclosing specimens of the Twopenny Blue stamp so that they might spot forgeries

TO ALL POSTMASTERS.

GENERAL POST OFFICE,
7th May, 1840.

REFERRING to the Circular of last Month, transmitting Specimens of the Penny and Twopenny Stamped Covers and Envelopes, and of the Penny Adhesive Labels, I now enclose *two Specimens of the Twopenny Adhesive Labels*, which you will preserve with the Specimens already sent to you, for the purpose of comparison with any doubtful Postage Stamps passing through your hands. I also enclose, for your information, two Specimens of the Label Stamp bearing the Letters V. R. at the upper corners, which are to be applied to the correspondence of Public Departments, and other Persons formerly enjoying the privilege of Official Franking. This latter Specimen of the Label Stamp is merely sent to prevent, when it may come into use, any misapprehension arising from the Letters V. R. which are intended to denote that the Stamp is employed for Official Correspondence.

I embrace this opportunity also of stating, it is at present understood that Postmasters and Letter Receivers will be required to sell *the Adhesive Label Stamps*, and the *Stamped Covers*, (but not the Envelopes) under Licence from the Commissioners of Stamps; upon this subject, however, you will receive full Instructions when the issue of Postage Stamps is extended to other Places than London.

By Command,

W. L. MABERLY,
SECRETARY.

will probably co-operate by looking up old records (which should contain names of early postmasters) and perhaps find some early date-stamps—always an exciting prospect—or specimen books of local cancellations going back to the opening of that particular post office.

Visits to all the sub-offices should be arranged and their simple stories uncovered. Here is where a camera is useful to have handy: the post office might be a picturesque one, or historical; there might be a Victorian pillar-box or wall-box worth photographing; the sub-postmaster/postmistress might be an interesting character, with a story to tell or an unusual hobby to talk about.

Enquiries at the council offices might reveal the fact that there is an archivist attached to the council, or an historian in the district, and discreet requests for help in postal history matters might meet with a friendly response.

Then there are the early copies of the local paper. Here the Editor, if told of the project on hand, will allow old file copies to be consulted at the newspaper office. It is quite surprising how much postal news is recorded in early papers—probably much of it brief items, but all of value in building up the story of a local post. Going back to hints on sources of supply, it might be worth mentioning that, during the search for material, if an auction of the contents of a house takes place in the locality being studied, it is an idea to attend it.

Some years ago in a small Essex seaside town a jumble sale was organised in aid of a charity. Normally this would have been a quiet affair, with the residents and the inevitable dealer attending. But in this case word got around that Douglas Fairbanks Jr would put in an appearance, since he was spending a few days' holiday in the area. Like most famous Americans he had the natural, sentimental enthusiasm for simple things—and also an eye for an English antique that had a story to tell; particularly if in its purchase a good cause benefited. The charity in question did benefit from his presence, but so delighted was the crowd to see him there that some of the items announced by the auctioneer towards the end of the sale received little attention—including a large carton of early postcards, some with uncommon postmarks and many with Victorian views of houses, scenes and landmarks that had long since vanished—all a delight to the heart of a dectiologist. A local man, a collector of cards and postal history items, acquired the box of postcards for a few shillings.

Old Post office notices are today far more difficult to find than early theatre posters, and if any such notices are seen for sale in good condition at a reasonable price, they should be snapped up. But a word of warning: so popular

380 Wells Fargo 25 cent Pony Express stamp for ½-oz mail
381 Wells Fargo stamp for carrying one newspaper over Californian routes

382 The 5 cent blue stamp for mail carried by Samuel Archer King's balloon flights in Tennessee, USA, 1877
383 Cover from a Union artillery man, 1861
384 The first ever Christmas card, 1843

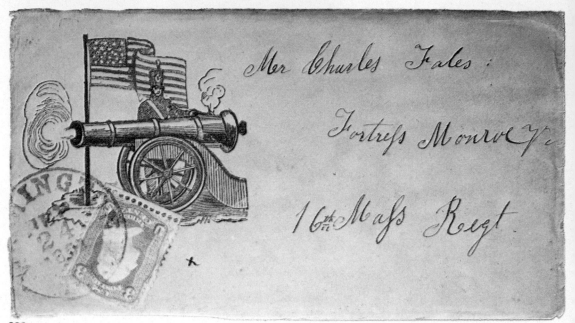

383

384

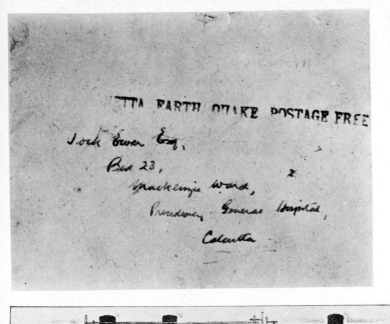

385 A cover from Quetta, where postage was free after the earthquake in 1935, because stamps were unavailable

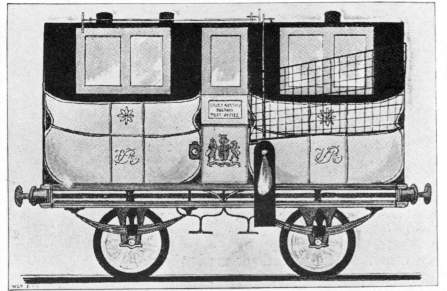

387

386 Mail coach tokens
387 An early travelling postal van, from the London and Birmingham railway
388 Old guns used in mail coach days

388

have these old notices become that some firms are now selling reproductions of them, and after a while these could find their way into old bookshops, etc and be offered, unwittingly it is hoped, as originals. A close examination of such posters will reveal whether it is an original or a modern product churned out by a good duplicating machine.

Early 19th century letters can still be obtained at reasonable prices. A bundle of perhaps twenty might be offered for as little as £1 because they appear to be of little importance; but the enquiring collector, with access to a good book on early postmarks, can often find some scarce markings in the otherwise common material. One such bundle bought by the author in auction for £2.50—there were 50 letters in all—contained ten York to Edinburgh/Leith letters, bearing the mark 'ADD ½' in a rectangle. Among the numerous regulations that cluttered up postal charges before Uniform Penny Postage swept many of them away, was the necessity for demanding an extra ½d on letters carried any distance in Scotland by mail coach. (Seven towns were exempt from the extra charge).

This particular mark is worth finding.

Free Franks

Postal markings known as Free Franks or Free Stamps make a fine study. Not a great deal has been written about them, so here is a field that should appeal to newcomers.

Free Franks may be collected in two states: the complete letter (entire) or the 'front' only. Naturally the former condition is preferable—and costs more. 'Fronts' are the result of a past generation of scissor-happy collectors trimming a latter sheet in such a manner that only the name, address and postal markings remained.

Fortunately for us, these scrap-book enthusiasts of the Georgian and early Victorian eras usually left quite a large portion of the front intact, so that today's collector has most of the essential information there to tell the story.

The 'fronts' were glued or pasted onto the pages of an album or scrap-book. Their value is considerably less than the complete letter sheet, but all are of value to present-day and future postal historians.

Prices of complete letters and 'fronts' vary according to the date of the markings, their clarity and the importance of the signatures. If the signature is that of a famous Member of Parliament or the House of Lords, then it also enters the Autograph category and has an enhanced value. An album containing about 100 'fronts' signed by 19th century MPs, whose names have little meaning today, and including a number of ordinary pre-stamp 'fronts', could be worth about £10. However,

the same number of items bearing the signatures of still famous men could have a value of well over £100.

Their origin

In 1660 Members of the English Parliament wanted a clause added to the Post Office Bill which would allow them to enjoy free postage. Jealous of this proposed privilege, the House of Lords objected. A settlement was eventually reached by a King's warrant whereby Members of Parliament *and* Peers, together with Officers of State, were permitted to send their mail free of charge while Parliament was sitting.

Then the fun started. Not content with this concession for themselves, many of those so privileged privately extended the benefits of the system to their constituents, friends and relations. It was quite simple to manipulate: those entitled to free postage merely signed on the front of the letter; this meant that they could write their names on blank sheets of paper and hand them to friends to use when they had a letter to write to someone.

In order to try to stop this abuse of the system, it was decreed in 1764 that signatories would have to write the complete address as well. But the losses to the Post Office through improper use of the franking system increased, as these figures show:

Loss in 1765—£51,000
Loss in 1772—£97,000
Loss in 1776—£119,000

Some further measures had to be taken to stop this loss, so the Post Office Act of 1784 decreed that Members, in their own handwriting, must add above the name and address the day, month and year, and the letter had to be posted on the day indicated.

Even these measures did not curtail the activities of those astute Members who were determined not to lose their self-created 'perks'. In manuscript they post-dated quantities of the franked sheets and presented them to their chosen friends for use on the date indicated.

If through ill-health a Member was unable to use the franking privilege himself, an Act of Parliament allowed him to appoint someone to act as his representative. But once again the temptation to take advantage of the system proved too strong for many. In April 1795 the House of Commons heard a case against a banker, Sir Benjamin Hammet, MP, who, when indisposed, delegated the franking of his letters to his son; but when he recovered his health he presumably forgot to cancel the arrangement, which went on for two years!

A fierce debate went on in the House, when other charges were made that a number of MPs, claiming illness, . . . had delegated their privilege of franking to their wives, daughters and other ladies.' Sir Benjamin emerged semi-

389 Pillar box designs in Great Britain.
1—3 are Guernsey and country pillar boxes of 1853—59; 4 and 5 are London and country standard designs of 1855—59;
6 and 7 are provincial non-standard designs, 1856—57; 8—10 are national standard and local versions of 1859—79; 11—13 show a reversion to cylindrical designs of 1879; 14 and 15 are modern designs

victorious in the voting that followed the debate; but an Act went through Parliament soon afterwards which decreed that a Member's franking should be limited to ten a day and that he be allowed to receive up to fifteen free of charge in one day. As a further measure, it was decreed that anyone who forged such franks was liable to be transported for seven years.

Part of the Free Franks story has been told here to show how delving into but one section of postal history can reveal a fascinating story.

This leads on to a lucky find the author made. Sorting through a lot of books 'double parked' in an old-fashioned bookcase in the home, a leather-bound volume was unearthed from the back row of a top shelf. This contained 150 Free Franks from almost every member of the House of Lords from 1823 to 1838. Whoever had built up this album had written on each page a brief description of the nobleman whose signature appeared on the face of the letter: George Spencer Churchill, Duke of Marlborough; William Spencer Cavendish, Duke of Devonshire; Arthur Wellesly, 1st Duke of Wellington—the pages of a history book were turned over in the mind with each page of that album, compiled so proudly by a devoted member of a family that had obviously known all the famous men concerned.

Although this particular album is a valuable record of postal significance, other such books must exist, perhaps not containing so many signatures of early aristocrats, but at least with a percentage of notable personalities. The gentlefolk of the 18th and 19th centuries were every bit as keen on forming collections of ephemera as we are today. Tucked away in bookcases and cupboards in the houses of old families are forgotten albums of crests, scrapbooks, letters, photographs, cards, all waiting to be found—and appreciated once again.

Maritime mail

This subject is a large one and as fresh and vigorous as the service it represents. Like most postal history it requires concentrated attention if success in it is to be achieved. Like all branches that make up the giant philatelic tree, there is much pioneer work still to be accomplished.

There is one modern writer who has made a magnificent contribution to maritime mail studies—Alan W. Robertson. Anyone who decides to build up a collection of this group should beg, borrow or buy *Maritime History of the British Isles* by Mr Robertson. This is such a monumental work that the demand for all the sections has made the purchase of the complete work rather expensive, but still a worthwhile investment.

There are other fine books to guide the collector in this fascinating subject, such as

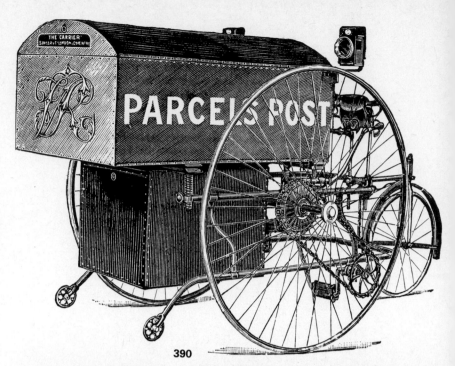

390

391

390 A parcel post tricycle carrier manufactured by Singer and Co at Coventry in the 1880s

391 A 'Hen and Chicken' bicycle used to speed up mails in the 1880s. Designed by an architect, it was like a 'Penny-farthing' on wheels, but it was awkward to handle and was replaced by the standard bicycle

392

392 A special ornamental envelope produced by the Junior Philatelic Society on the introduction of the Anglo-American Penny Post

393 A cover celebrating the arrival at Houston, Texas, of Charles Lindbergh, who flew the Atlantic single-handed. It bears the 'Kicking Horse' cancellation and the commemorative stamp shows his aircraft *Spirit of St Louis*

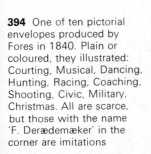
393

394 One of ten pictorial envelopes produced by Fores in 1840. Plain or coloured, they illustrated: Courting, Musical, Dancing, Hunting, Racing, Coaching, Shooting, Civic, Military, Christmas. All are scarce, but those with the name 'F. Deraedemaeker' in the corner are imitations

111

Frank Staff's *Transatlantic Mail,* and recently *Ships of the Channel Islands* by Richard Mayne.

When any of the important books relating to the development of sea mail appear in the literature sections of auctions, it would be a wise move to buy them.

Research

A well-known postal historian, Leonard E. Britnor, builds up some of his studies from research work done in the Records Office of the Post Office, St Martins-le-Grand, London EC1. In this efficiently-run department there are large files of old documents and letters relating to British and Overseas postal services. The student is thus able to make comprehensive notes on the early postmasters, post-boys, mail coach routes and time-tables. For the person with the available time and the ability to extract information from a mass of material, some of it perhaps a little dull reading, much of of it undiscovered excitement, then this Records Office is a treasure house. But a gentle warning: one must be methodical and know what to look for in order to derive the most benefit from this service—a service that is free, for which we have to thank the Post Office and the courteous employees in 'Records'.

The previously-mentioned Mr Britnor has listed for us some of the main sections, which should act as a guide for the new student.

Postmaster General's Minutes, 1794 to date.
Postmaster General's Reports 1791–1841.
Packet Minutes, 1811–1920.
Packet Reports, 1807–1837.
Post Office Notices, from 1681, but chiefly 1790–1900.
Treasury Minutes, Letters, Accounts, 1686 to date.
Commission Books, 1759–1854.
Staff, Establishment, 1742 to date.
Inland Mails, organisation, 1652 to date; services, 1690 to date.
Overseas Mail, organisation, 1675 to date; services, parcel post, air mails, 1856 to date; contracts, 1755–1888.
Telecommunications, 1846 to date.
Die impressions, 1825 to date.
Collections of private papers:
Col. Roger Whitley, Deputy PMG, 1662–1677.
Sir Thomas Frankland, Joint PMG, 1694–1697.
Lord Walsingham, Joint PMG, 1762–1792.
John Palmer, Surveyor, 1775–1845.
Sir Francis Freeling, Secretary, 1796–1836.
Marquis of Salisbury, Joint PMG, 1820–1823.
Sir Rowland Hill, Secretary, 1839–1869.
John Tilley, Secertary, 1853–1874.

Most reliable authors, when setting out to write a book on the postal history of some

395 An unaccepted design for the Robert Burns commemorative issue of 1966
396 The 1/3 value of the Robert Burns commemorative issue of 1966. The portrait is that by Nasmyth
397 The 4d value Burns stamp shows the poet from a chalk drawing of Skirving
398 Sudanese stamps of 1898 incorporating the drawing shown on the right
399 The original sketch by a member of Lord Kitchener's staff for Sudanese stamps. Khartoum and Berber were written lightheartedly on the mailbags, even though Berber was at the time in enemy hands. There was consternation when it was discovered that De la Rue had incorporated both place names in microscopic letters on the actual stamps. However, Berber was recaptured by the time the stamps were issued

395

398

399

396

397

district or country, go to the 'direct source' for information. Thus, a town's early historical records are consulted, any correspondence of old families searched for—in fact, the author becomes a Sherlock Holmes in his search for facts. If the reader would like to see how this planning works to perfection, a good example is *Three Centuries of Scottish Posts* by A. R. B. Haldane, published in 1971 by the Edinburgh University Press, George Square, Edinburgh.

Postal history is such a vast subject that most collectors limit their activities to a particular country—usually that in which they are domiciled. Thus the American normally chooses USA, the Britisher, Great Britain, the German, Germany and so on.

Today the demand for material is so intense that, unfortunately, prices are rising. But the collector who reads up the chosen subject is the one who has the knowledge to recognise bargains in unexpected places.

A lot of practical knowledge is acquired by joining in the activities of a club devoted to postal history. Some stamp societies have a postal history section, and in most countries there is at least one group devoted exclusively to the subject. In England there is the Postal History Society (Secretary: W. Raife Wellsted, 23 Shelley Close Langley, Bucks); the Society of Postal Historians (V. Denis Vanderveldge 25 Sinclair Grove, London NW11); East Anglia Postal History Study Circle and the Essex Postal History Group (G. P. Green, Bretaye, Mill Hill, Shenfield, Essex); Forces Postal History (W. Garrard, 7 Hillbick Way, Greenford, Middlesex); London Postal History Group (M. M. English, 50 Somerden Road, Orpington, Kent); Polish Postal History Society of Great Britain (H. E. J. Evans, Court House, Court Lane, Cosham, Portsmouth, Hants).

Most stamp periodicals feature articles on the subject, and there are a number of society journals devoted to the study of the posts. 1972 saw the launching of *Postal History International*, published monthly by Proud-Bailey Co Ltd, 98 Queens Road, Brighton.

To list important works on British postal history would take close on 20 pages of this book. Fortunately the subject has now been covered in *A List of Books on the Postal History, Postmarks and Adhesive Postage and Revenue Stamps of Great Britain*, by Arnold Strange, published by The Great Britain Philatelic Society Publications, Watford, Herts.

The mail arriving at Temple Bar in 1834. From a coloured
print by permission of Messrs. J. H. and J. Brooke

Societies, exhibitions, literature

FANCY SNUFF & CIGAR WAREHOUSE

The real pleasure to be obtained from all kinds of collecting is in showing one's possessions to others. A joy shared is indeed a joy trebled. Societies offer many amenities, one of the most important of which is the opportunity given to members to see fine collections, to study them from a critical and comparison point of view and to benefit from the knowledge gained.

The friendships made at meetings can be lifelong, which proves the truth of the thought that a collector is never lonely.

Everyone should belong to at least one society—some avid collectors boast membership of ten!—for a society keeps the hobby active, up-to-date and youthful. If one goes to almost any meeting there will be found a group of happy men and women, enthusiastic about their own and other people's pet subjects, keen to help others, and when it is a question of taking office in an honorary capacity, entering into the administration or organising activities with an energy and enthusiasm sometimes lacking when it comes to their paid jobs!

For the young collector membership of a society is essential to successful collecting. For the business man or woman the relaxation and companionship of a society is invaluable as a means of unwinding after the tension of a week or more spent in the battle of commercial life.

There are societies to suit the tastes of every kind of collector—general, specialised, Cinderella. No difficulty should be experienced by the lone collector in finding a suitable society, for today there is one in almost every town, large or small.

An important point to remember about all societies is that a visitor is always welcome, so that if there are a number of societies that interest a collector, the thing to do is write to each secretary and ask for an invitation to attend a meeting at which there is a display; the collector will soon find the society with the most personal appeal.

And for addresses of secretaries and meeting places? Local community centres and libraries should be able to help here; also local weekly newspapers should know the locations of all hobbies clubs, since they often report their activities. In Great Britain there is the British Philatelic Association, to which nearly all societies in the country belong; they publish the BPA Year Book containing details of member-societies, which are also sub-divided into areas, so it is a simple matter to select a conveniently located society. The Association's address is 446 Strand, London WC2.

There are some collectors who try to get along without the help of a society; it is false economy, for they limit their activities and enjoyment by such isolation. Yet, why *should* member-

ship of an organised body of collectors be so important? We believe that the companionship of fellow enthusiasts is essential for the full appreciation of any hobby. The competitive element acts as an incentive, so that in a spirit of friendly rivalry the individual collector sets out to prove that with a little skill, observation and searching for elusive items he or she can emerge as a philatelist of some importance in a particular sphere.

Many societies conduct a club or exchange packet, composed usually of booklets 5" × 8" containing 12 or more plain pages. Members buy these from the society or elsewhere and mount their duplicate stamps in them, priced—usually below catalogue value. The 'packet superintendent' collects 20 or more of these booklets and despatches them in a cardboard box to the first member of the 'circuit', who takes out the stamps that are wanted, signs the blank space and then sends the packet to the next name on the list of members. The money for stamps taken is despatched to the superintendent.

This method is ideal for disposing of duplicates (except the very common stamps) and for buying stamps cheaply.

Societies are great fun. They open up a new world for the lonely collector; they give confidence to the person taking up the hobby; encourage the shy collector to take an active part in club life and it is not long before the congenial atmosphere of meetings inspires the 'quiet one' to give a display and a talk. It is a known fact that many a collector, too shy even to second a vote of thanks at a meeting, has been coaxed into showing a few items at a combined members' display, and has gone on to take up a whole evening with a personal show, eventually emerging as a popular speaker, sought after by other societies.

Showing the stamps

While complete uniformity in the presentation of philatelic material for private display and public exhibition purposes would be very monotonous, there are certain standards to which displays should conform if the hope of the owner is to be recognised as a serious philatelist.

First, a few mistakes to avoid.

Overcrowding: too many stamps on a page make it look like an old-fashioned dealer's approval sheet. If there are more than a dozen stamps on a page the eye gets impatient.

Since a picture is worth a thousand words, there are illustrated on page 119 three examples of good layout.

Inferior specimens: any that are badly torn, or look as if they had been kept in a schoolboy's pocket along with some half-eaten toffee, or are very badly postmarked; these are best thrown away. Better to have a blank space on a

400 Medal presented by the Royal Philatelic Society of London at international exhibitions
401 Her Majesty the Queen meets Fellows of the Royal Philatelic Society during their centenary celebrations

402 The Hungarian artist Eva Gabor colouring one of her drawings for the 1960 Fairy Tales issue. A theme presented at exhibitions can be enhanced by having as a 'frontispiece' a large drawing of one of the designs
403–406 Four of the 1959 issue of Hungarian Fairy Tales stamps designed by Eva Gabor

407 The Silver Jubilee of the Association of Essex Philatelic Societies in 1969 was marked by the famous Essex postmark of 1674 being incorporated into a modern cancellation used on correspondence on a mail coach run

page than spoil its appearance with a grubby stamp. The only excuse for harbouring a poor looking specimen is if it is a rarity.

Some people are against mixing mint and used together in sets. This is a matter of taste—and availability of specimens. There is no valid reason why a mint stamp should not 'stand in' to complete a row until a postmarked specimen turns up, just as a nicely used stamp can fill a gap while waiting for a mint stamp to come on the scene.

In a thematic collection unused are best, or failing that specimens very lightly cancelled or just 'tipped' on the corner so that the centre design is not obscured.

Stamps arranged in the black horizontal strips with clear front protection are often used these days. The strip, which is gummed on the back, is cut to the required length, stuck down on the album page and the stamps inserted under the clear front. The trouble with some of these strips is that stamps can move if the page is jolted.

This strip idea came about through the 'unmounted mint' fetish that swept through the philatelic world some years ago. Certain dealers were partly responsible: while they sold at a fair price unused stamps that had traces of having been mounted, when they themselves came to buy unused stamps from a collector they insisted on 'unmounted mint'—otherwise the price offered was usually low. This made many collectors afraid to use mounts on their mint stamps, so the 'strips' became popular.

The term 'unmounted mint' is a misnomer: a mint stamp is one that is as fresh and un-marked as the day it came from the printers.

Broadly speaking, the condition of a stamp can be divided into: used, unused, mint. The first two terms can be sub-divided into a number of states, but not the latter. As soon as a mint stamp receives a mount on its gummed side, or becomes very slightly faded through exposure to strong light or climatic conditions, then it enters the 'unused' category.

Some final remarks on this 'unmounted mint' craze. The gum on the back of a stamp has always been a sticky problem for collectors in more senses than one. In the early days the majority of stamps were secured to the album page by means of gum, or, as collecting methods improved, large pieces of stamp edging. Many specimens became valuable and when eventually removed from the old pages the once unused stamps were, not unnaturally, minus gum. Some collectors in tropical climates remove the gum from mint specimens before putting them in albums, for it is better to have no gum on the backs than a collection of once mint stamps firmly stuck on the album page through a humid atmosphere.

408 The Duke of Bedford examines the Crown Agents' display at a Woburn Abbey stamp exhibition

409 An example of writing up. A Harrison Great Britain Universal Post Union set of 1949 on a presentation card

408

409

BOMBAY CIRCLE

TYPE 4ᴴ

LETTER WRITTEN BY THE SECRETARY OF THE BANK OF BOMBAY FROM BOMBAY TO BAGHDAD, TURKISH ARABIA. DATED 8ᴛʜ JULY 1863.

THIS LETTER TRAVELLED TO BAGHDAD VIA THE DESERT ROUTE. ALTHOUGH BY 1862 A REGULAR SIX-WEEKLY MAIL SERVICE TO THE PERSIAN GULF WAS PERFORMED BY THE BRITISH INDIA STEAM NAVIGATION COMPANY WITH MAIL CONVEYED TO BAGHDAD BY THE EUPHRATES AND TIGRIS STEAM NAVIGATION COMPANY FROM BASRAH, THIS LETTER WAS SENT VIA THE RED SEA.

THE ROUTE ACTUALLY TRAVELLED FROM BOMBAY WENT DOWN THE RED SEA TO SUEZ FROM WHERE IT WENT OVERLAND TO ALEXANDRIA - NOTE BACKSTAMP "ALEXANDRIA/A/AU 4/63" IN A 19ᴍᴍ CIRCLE. FROM ALEXANDRIA THE LETTER WAS CARRIED BY SHIP TO BEYROUT WHERE IT PICKED UP THE DESERT ROUTE TO BAGHDAD VIA DAMASCUS. BY THIS ROUND-ABOUT ROUTE, LETTERS TOOK FROM FORTY TO FORTY-FIVE DAYS TO REACH BAGHDAD.

AT THIS DATE, NO POST OFFICE EXISTED IN BAGHDAD, AND THE CONSULATE ACTED AS THE CENTRE FOR RECEIPT AND DESPATCH OF LETTERS.

410 Presenting for exhibition a letter written by the Secretary Treasurer of the Bank of Bombay and sent in July 1863 to Baghdad via the desert route. All relevant facts are neatly laid out

411–413 Three pages from a thematic collection by Margaret Morris 'Astronomy' which won the Link House Silver Cup at the British Philatelic Exhibition in 1971

410

Introduction

From earliest times man has observed the ever-changing spectacle of the heavens, wondering, and attempting to explain and to understand.

Ancient Astronomy

The Aztecs had an advanced knowledge of astronomy developed mainly because of their very complicated religion. The calendar was at the base of every action of the Aztecs and their lives were regulated by it.

Space Research

Since the launching of Sputnik I on 4ᵗʰ October 1957, there have been many successful space probes providing information useful to astronomy.

It is known that over the years certain gum, especially in hot climates, can adversely affect the paper—and so the colour—of a stamp. Little wonder, then, that the philatelist is beginning to question the advisability of worrying about the gum problem, particularly as the analytical chemist has stated that if rare unused stamps are to be preserved for future generations, then the mucilage should be carefully washed off!

Being an independent type of species, collectors will decide for themselves whether to use mounts or not on mint stamps. But let us end on this thought: some years ago, when there was a sudden boom in current commemorative stamps, a lot of people—mostly non-collectors—decided to climb on the bandwagon and 'invest' in sheets of stamps and hundreds of modern mint sets 'preserved' in packets. When they thought the time was right they started to unload them on the market. The result was unfortunate for many such 'investors', and the hobby suffered for a while from the activities of these 'mad mint mugs' as they were sometimes called.

Stamp collecting *can* be an excellent investment; but first and foremost it is a hobby to be enjoyed by the true collector.

Exhibitions

Three of the main factors that keep the hobby so alive are: magazines, societies, exhibitions. Probably the latter attract more recruits than anything else. Exhibitions can be divided into three categories: local, national, international. The local ones are happening almost every day in town and village; the London nationals are the annual Stampex, at the Royal Horticultural Hall, Westminster SW1, and the British Philatelic Exhibition, Seymour Place W1. An international usually takes place in a particular country every ten years. All exhibitions, from that in the village hall to the big internationals, are thrilling to attend.

Literature

To obtain full benefit from the hobby, it is essential for the collector to read about it, talk about it and see how other people show their material. As has been said, important facets of philately are literature, societies and exhibitions. Without them the hobby would fade out. A well-read collector gets the most enjoyment from the hobby, gives the best displays and wins the most awards at exhibitions. This sounds rather like an advertisement, which it is—for literature.

The books, pamphlets and magazines on the hobby are its life blood. No one can collect successfully without the guidance of such publications. Having said that, let us now describe a small collection of useful reference books. No two such collections will be the same, for each will reflect the particular branch of philately which is favoured by the owner. Catalogues will be the most frequently consulted volumes, and here the choice is wide. Great Britain, France, Germany, Switzerland and the USA all produce large volumes in two or three parts listing the issues of the world. They are all essential works, carefully produced and usually appearing annually.

Specialised works of many countries are published regularly. Some of them may be expensive, but if it is hoped to become an expert on a subject then the money spent will be an investment.

A guide to the hobby is also a necessity, not only for the beginner but for the more advanced collector who needs to check general facts now and again. The choice is not easy, since hundreds of such books have been published in the English language alone; but here are some suggestions:

The Illustrated Encyclopedia of Stamp Collecting by Otto Hornung. Hamlyn Publishing Group Ltd, Feltham, Middlesex, 1970.

Stamp Collecting by Stanley J. Phillips. Stanley Gibbons Ltd, London.

Postage Stamps in the Making by Fred J. Melville. Stanley Gibbons Ltd, London. This is almost a classic; a wonderful book first published in 1916 and later revised in 1949 by John Easton. Second-hand copies of the original work sometimes turn up in auctions—and it is a very scarce book.

An up-to-date work that goes thoroughly into the production of postage stamps (it took 15 years to write) is *Fundamentals of Philately* by L. N. and M. Williams. This is obtainable in one volume, published by The American Philatelic Society, PO Box 800, State College, Pa 16801, USA. It is available in England from the main philatelic literature distributors.

One of the most ambitious literary projects in the philatelic world, now brought to a successful conclusion, has been *The International Encyclopedia of Stamps*. This consists of six volumes, each of 14 parts, with a special self-binder for each volume. It is almost a library on its own, but as philately is so comprehensive this work should be treated like any good encyclopedia—each classified entry an introduction to a vast subject.

Literature on one's own speciality should form the basis of a small personal library—by 'library' we mean, of course, a large bookcase! If the speciality is Great Britain, America, Australia or one of the big European countries, then the choice of reading matter is enormous and some restraint has to be exercised, or duplication of the subject will occur. A specialised catalogue on the chosen country is essential, augmented by one of the recognised standard works that takes an overall look at the subject.

416 Many big exhibitions produce commemorative souvenir sheets; these have no postal use but are often of value to a collector. The Stampex 1963 sheet showed six-colour separations of the $20 Hong Kong of 1962

Six-colour separations of the $20 Hong Kong issue, 1962. The head of the Queen is taken from a portrait by Pietro Annigoni. Stamps printed by permission of the Postmaster-General, Hong Kong and by courtesy of the Crown Agents, to commemorate Britain's National Stamp Exhibition

STAMPEX 1963 MARCH 15-23
CENTRAL HALL, WESTMINSTER, LONDON, S.W.1.
HARRISON & SONS LTD. LONDON   POSTAGE STAMPS REPRODUCED BY PERMISSION OF THE POSTMASTER-GENERAL

THE IDEAL STAMP.

An enlarged reproduction of the "Ideal" Stamp which is being printed and perforated at the Jubilee International Stamp Exhibition.

414 An enlarged reproduction in the form of a postcard of the 'Ideal' Stamp printed and perforated at the Jubilee Stamp Exhibition in London 1912

415 The first catalogue published in the United States by J. W. Scott and Co, September 1868. Penny Blacks of Great Britain were priced at 5 cents!

DESCRIPTIVE CATALOGUE
OF
American and Foreign
Postage Stamps,

ISSUED
FROM
1840
TO DATE,

SPLENDIDLY   WITH COLORED

ILLLUSTRATED   ENGRAVINGS.

AND
Containing the Current Value of each Variety.

PRICE 15 CENTS.

NEW YORK:
PUBLISHED BY J. W. SCOTT & CO.,
WHOLESALE AND RETAIL DEALERS IN
FOREIGN POSTAGE STAMPS,
34 LIBERTY STREET.

SEPTEMBER, 1868.

Entered according to Act of Congress, in the year 1868, by J. W. SCOTT & CO., in the Clerk's Office of the District Court of the United States for the Southern District of New York.

Wm. B. Smyth, Printer,-4 New Chambers St., N. Y.

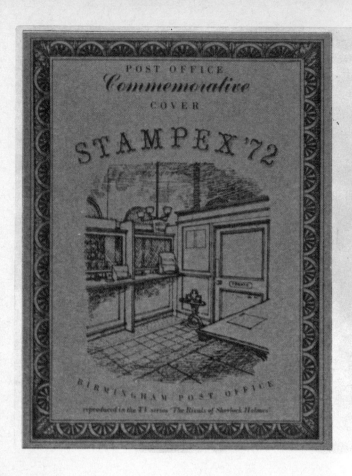

The Amateur Collector Limited,
Royal Horticultural Hall,
Greycoat & Elverton Streets,
LONDON, S.W.1.

417 The commemorative cover issued for the Stampex 72 exhibition

To get a good coverage of a selected country, it is often necessary to acquire a number of books to embrace postal history, general issues, locals, fiscals, postmarks etc. If a guiding hand is needed in the selection of the essential books in a complicated group, the librarian of one of the big societies should be consulted. If it is found that most of the books required are in the library, then membership of that particular society is the answer to the problem. Some people do not favour borrowing books— they like to own them so that they can underline passages and write notes on the pages if necessary and always have the book at hand to browse through. For these independent people, it is best to consult a philatelic books supplier or the Editor of a magazine, both of whom should know of new and forthcoming books. Most magazines feature regular book reviews and carry advertisements of the latest works published.

Libraries

As has been said, society libraries can help collectors in search of special books; societies also have complete 'runs' of most magazines, early and current. But where to find these libraries and how accessible are they?

Most general libraries in large and small towns have a shelf devoted to hobbies, and here may be found catalogues and some books on stamps. Through an inter-departmental system, libraries borrow volumes from a central source, an interchange scheme that gives a small library access to a very wide range of books on all subjects.

One of the greatest private philatelic libraries formed many years ago was that of the Earl of Crawford. Now known as the Crawford Library, it is housed in the British Museum and the books are available in the normal way. Many are not listed in the Museum's *General Catalogue of Printed Books*, so the *Catalogue of the Philatelic Library of the Earl of Crawford* by Sir Edward Bacon should be consulted for any book required. Many other books and periodicals, both English and Foreign, are in the General catalogue under author (books) and title (periodicals). Modern material from 1965 is not yet fully catalogued, but is contained in a card index on Bar K in the Reading Room.

The National Postal Museum in King Edward Street, near St Pauls, London, is building up a useful collection of literature for the use of students.

The construction of a permanent home for the American Philatelic Society Research Library and the National Headquarters of the APS started in State College, Pa in the Autumn of 1971. The Philatelic Research Library, organised in 1969, became fully operational in 1972. It occupies the first floor of the building and research material is now available to collectors everywhere. Rare volumes are kept in vaults on the first floor and other scarce material on the second floor.

418 Exhibitions have a wide appeal—this lady is at the British Philatelic Exhibition

Another magnificent collection of books, and periodicals, is owned by the Collector's Club in New York. This is acknowledged by many to be the premier philatelic library in America. Every year the library adds close on 2,000 items to its shelves—little wonder that space on the second floor has been exhausted and that an Archive Section has been started in a basement room in which to keep the less consulted volumes. A courteous service is offered to members of this top American club. The address is 22 East 35th Street, New York, NY 10016, USA.

In 1972 Sussex University in England, set in a beautiful park near Brighton, added a considerable amount of material to its library. This University's philatelic unit is luxuriously appointed and its Director, Professor John West, is a prominent philatelist who is promoting philately in the University.

The largest society library in Great Britain is that housed at 41 Devonshire Place, London W1, the headquarters of the Royal Philatelic Society. Three rooms and a storage basement contain books, pamphlets, auction catalogues and bound magazines from the early days right through to current issues. Nearly all the rarities of philatelic literature are packed into these few rooms.

The National Philatelic Society at 44 Fleet Street, London EC4, possesses a good general library, but like that of the Royal Philatelic Society, only members may use the facilities offered.

Magazines

There are more periodicals published on stamp collecting than on any other hobby.

Over 300 make their regular appearance in the philatelic world: weekly, monthly, quarterly or yearly. The important ones range from a high quality 'glossy', to study circle bulletins, in every major language. America tops the list with about 80 publications. A British monthly has a 60,000 circulation and an American weekly has one even higher. Combined readership runs into millions.

Considering the great number published, mortalities among the magazines are few; many are old-established, such as the *Philatelic Journal of Great Britain*, since 1891, and new ones still apear such as the *Postal History International* in 1972.

The following list is based on magazines printed in the English language, which the author receives regularly.

(Ref: w=weekly; m=monthly; qr=quarterly; y=yearly).

Great Britain

Aero Field (m). Sutton Coldfield.
Cinderella Philatelist (m). Cinderella Stamp Club London NW11.
Courier (m). Post Office, London EC1.
London Philatelist (11 issues per year). Royal Philatelic Society, London W1.
Maple Leaves (bi-m). Canadian Philatelic Society of Great Britain, Rotherham, Yorkshire.
Philatelic Bulletin (m). Post Office, London EC1.
Philatelic Journal of Great Britain (qr). Robson Lowe Ltd, London SW1.
Philatelic Magazine (m). London WC2.
Philatelist (m). Robson Lowe Ltd, London SW1.
Philately (bi-m). British Philatelic Association, London WC2.
Postal History The Postal History Society, London.
Postal History International (m). Proud-Bailey, Brighton.
Railway Philately (qr). Railway Philatelic Group, Kirby-in-Ashfield, Nottingham.
Stamp Collecting (w). London WC2.
Stamp Lover (bi-m). National Philatelic Society, London EC4.
Stamp Magazine (m). Link House Publications Ltd, Croydon, Surrey.
Stamp Monthly (m). Stanley Gibbons Ltd, London WC2.
Stamp Year Book (y). Link House Publications Ltd, Croydon, Surrey.

Australia

Australian Stamp Monthly (m). Horticultural Press Pty Ltd, Melbourne, Victoria.

Philately from Australia (qr). Royal Philatelic Society, Victoria.
Stamp News (m). Review Publications Pty Ltd, Dubbo, NSW.

Canada

Canadian Philatelist (m). Ontario.

India

India's Stamp Journal (m). Bombay.
Philatelic Journal of India (m). Fort Bombay.
Stamp Digest (m). Calcutta.

South Africa

South African Philatelist (m). The Philatelic Federation of Southern Africa, Johannesburg.

United States of America

American Philatelist (m). American Philatelic Society, Phoenix, Arizona.
Collectors Club Philatelist (m). The Collectors Club, New York.
HJMR Newslist. Philatelic Literature (bi-m). North Miami, Florida.
Linn's Stamp News (w). The Sydney Printing and Publishing Co, Sydney, Ohio.
Mekeel's Weekly Stamp News (w). Severn-Wylie-Jewett Co, Maine.
Minkus Stamp Journal (qr). New York.
National Stamp News (3 issues a month). The National Philatelic Society, Anderson, South Carolina.
Philatelic Literature Review (qr). Philatelic Literature Association, Canajoharie, New York.
SPA Journal (m). Society of Philatelic Americans, Cincinnati, Ohio.
Scott Monthly Journal (m). Scott Publishing Co, Omaha, Nebraska.
Stamps (w). H. L. Lindquist Publications Inc, New York, NY
Topical Times (bi-m). American Topical Association, Milwaukee, Wis.
Western Stamp Collector (w). Van Dahl Publications Inc, Oregon.

Details of all publications not listed above, together with those in foreign languages, may be obtained from *Stamp Year Book*, Link House, Dingwall Ave, Croydon, CR9 2TA, or HJMR Co, PO Box 308, North Miami, Florida 33161, USA.

Conclusion

When any writer finishes a book on stamps and reads his completed manuscript for the last time before it is whisked off to the printers, he is always conscious that much has been left unsaid.

This feeling is common to all philatelic authors, but recognised as inevitable because of the immensity and wide range of the subject.

How many different entries under countries in the catalogue are there to consider—1,700?

How many interesting stamps whose background should be told—160,000?

How many branches of the hobby worthy of serious study—25?

How many excellent books that the Complete Philatelist should know about—500?

So the many groups that make the hobby such an immense one for the collector—and the trader—demand to be recognised by the writer of a general book. What can he do but select some for special mention, because they are so very important, and hope that a brief reference to others will inspire the reader to seek 'further reading'.

And finally, a few random thoughts on the hobby.

When youngsters take it up and—despite so many other attractions—continue with it through their student days, they automatically and unconsciously absorb a knowledge of many places, people and events that proves of value in their future careers.

It can also be claimed, without fear of contradiction, that the man or woman who becomes absorbed in philately finds relaxation in it and an escape from the stress of modern life.

For those leading a quieter existence stamps keep them up-to-date with world affairs and impart the feeling that they are still active—which they are, or they would not be collecting stamps!

Unlike the material of many hobbies, stamps are so portable—a favourite album may be put in a suitcase during a business trip or a holiday, and blank spaces noted afresh when, during the travels, a dealer is found in a town being visited. A much-wanted stamp picked up by a collector when away on vacation is always more thrilling than the same specimen bought on home ground.

The 'brotherhood of philately' is no loose term. It represents a friendly hand extended to all collectors everywhere, through personal contact in a busy philatelic society or the world-wide correspondence stamp exchange club for the lone collector, such as that organised by a certain magazine in Britain.

Within recent years there has been a big increase in the number of the fair sex entering what was once the man's world of philately. They have brought a fresh outlook to some sections of the hobby: their attendance at exhibitions and society meetings brightens up the atmosphere considerably. Their presence has met with no opposition from the male, in fact they have been welcomed with open arms . . .

With this happy thought we shall end our book.

Appendix

Stamps in museums

British Museum, Great Russell Street, London WC1. Contains the famous Tapling, Mosely, Fitzgerald airmails and the Bojanowicz Polish Collections.

Bruce Castle, Lordship Lane, Tottenham, London N17. A fine, expanding collection, strong in postal history. (Not open Wednesday or Sunday.)

British Red Cross,14 Grosvenor Crescent, London SW1. A large collection of Red Cross stamps, mounted in a special cabinet. Viewed by appointment.

Birmingham City Museum and Art Gallery, Congreve Street, Birmingham 3. A permanent all-world collection of value, and occasional displays of specialised collections.

Halifax (Yorkshire), Bankfield Museum and Art Gallery, Akroyd Park. A good collection of British material.

Imperial War Museum, Lambeth Road, London SE1. A large collection of World War 1 stamps in cabinets. World War 1 and 2 covers, leaflets, etc, and World War 2 stamps now being arranged for public display. Viewed by appointment.

National Maritime, Romney Road, Greenwich, London, SE10. The Frank Staff collection of covers and material associated with Trans-Atlantic Mail.

National Postal, London Chief Office, King Edward Street, London EC1. The world's finest collection of Great Britain, including the famous Reginald Phillips collection from the Penny Black to 1901; the Berne whole world collection of over 200,000 specimens; postal history; thematics, air mails.

Science Museum, Exhibition Road, South Kensington, London SW7. The Penn-Gaskell aerophilatelic collection: stamps, covers, posters, watches and fans decorated with ballooning scenes, etc. As some of the material is stored in albums, requests to view should be sent to the Keeper of the Aviation Section.

Expert committees

Certificates of genuineness of stamps and philatelic material may be obtained from groups of experts for a fee. Details of the services offered may be obtained from the following:

British Philatelic Association, 446 Strand, London WC2.
National Philatelic Society, 44 Fleet Street, London EC4.
Royal Philatelic Society, 41 Devonshire Place, London W1.
Philatelic Information Bureau, 30 Dunstan Road, London NW11.
(Identification of 'Cinderella' material and tracing mystery specimens.)

Trade organisations

American Stamp Dealers Association, Inc. 147 West 42nd Street, New York, NY 10036, USA.
British Philatelic Association, 446 Strand, London WC2.
Philatelic Traders' Society, 27 John Adam Street, London WC2

Trade publications

ASDA Bulletin, 147 West 42nd Street, New York, NY 10036, USA.
Philatelic Exporter, PO Box No. 4, Edgware, Middlesex.
Philatelic Trader, 42 Maiden Lane, London WC2.
PTS Journal, 27 John Adam Street, London WC2.
Stamp Wholesaler, PO Box 529, Burlington, Vt. USA.

Philatelic bureaux

(Complete lists appear in *International Stamp Dealers' Directory* 1970, and Stamp Year Book 1972.)
Australia, PO Box 259, South Melbourne, Australia 3205.
Austria, Director General, Posts and Telegraphs A-1011, Postgasse 8, Vienna.

Bangladesh, Philatelic Agency, Cobham, Woking, Surrey; or Inter-Governmental Philatelic Corp, 225 West 34th Street, Pennsylvania Building, New York 1, NY, USA.
Belgium, Administration of Posts, Service to Collectors, 1000, Brussels.
British Commonwealth, Crown Agents, St Nicholas House, St. Nicholas Road, Sutton, Surrey.
Canada, Philatelic Service, Canada Post Office, Ottawa 8, Canada.
China (Formosa), Director General of Posts, Philatelic Department, Taipei, Taiwan 106.
Cook Islands, PO Box 200, Rarotonga, Cook Islands.
Cyprus, Ministry of Communications, Department of Posts, Nicosia.
Czechoslovakia, Artia, Philatelic Department, PO Box 790, Prague 1.
Finland, General Direction of PTT, Simonkatu 12Z, PO Box 654, 10100 Helsinki 10.
Germany (East), Global Gen-Nr 00023 uber Postkontroll-Amt, Kst Deutscher Buch-Export u Import, GmbH, Leipzig.
Germany (West), Der Bundesminsterium fur das Post u Fernmeldewesen, 53 Bonn 1, Postfach, 80 01.
Great Britain, 2–4 Waterloo Place, Edinburgh, Scotland.
Greece, Hellenic Post, 1 Apellou Street, Athens 111.
Guernsey, Head Post Office, Guernsey, Channel Islands.
Holland, PTT, Prinses Beatrixlaan 11, 's-Gravenhage.
Hungary, Philatelia Hungarica, PO Box 600, Budapest 5.
India, Office of the Director General, PTT, New Delhi.
Ireland (Eire), Department of Posts and Telegraphs, Dublin 1.
Israel, Ministry of Posts, Philatelic Services, GPO Building, Jerusalem.
Japan, Tokyo Central PO, Tokyo 100.
Jersey, Philatelic Service of the Postal Administration, PO Box, 304, Jersey, Channel Islands.
New Zealand, Post Office Headquarters, Private Bag, Wellington.
Pakistan, The Manager, Philatelic Bureau, GPO, Karachi.
Poland, Ruch, PO Box 1001, Warsaw 1.
Rhodesia, Philatelic Bureau, Private Bag 199H, Salisbury.
Russia, Philatelic Department, Moscow G 200, USSR.
South Africa, Philatelic Bureau, GPO Pretoria.
Sweden, Postens Filateliavdelning PFA, Fack, S-101 10, Stockholm 1.
United Nations, Postal Administration, Palais des Nations, Geneva 10.
United States of America, PO Department, Washington DC 20260.

International clubs

The 'Big Four' with world-wide membership:
American Philatelic Society, PO Box 800, State College, Pa 16801, USA.
Collectors Club, 22 East 35th Street, New York, NY 10016, USA.
Royal Philatelic Society, 41 Devonshire Place, London W1.
National Philatelic Society, 44 Fleet Street, London EC4

Philatelic charity

Action for the Crippled Child (National Fund for the Research into Crippling Diseases), Capt Alan Clark, ACTION, Vincent House, Vincent Square, London SW1. This charity welcomes gifts of loose stamps, collections, albums, books. Stamps and special first day covers are also sold to collectors to raise funds. Details on application.

Index

Numbers in italics refer to illustrations

Albums 40
–for booklets 50
–for covers 93
American Bank Note Co 33
American Philatelic Society 80, 122
American Topical Association 80
Archer, Henry 24, 26, 30
Australia
–group collecting 53 *et seq*
–stamps *53–55, 73, 77*
Australian Post Office 54

Bangladesh stamps *40, 41*
Barnard, James 20
Beeching envelope *18*
Belgium stamps *79*
Bellman *19*
Bhutan stamps 26, *27*
Bicycle posts *110*
Billets Post Paye 16
Bishop, Colonel Henry 11, *11*, 12, 97
Bishop marks *11*, 12, 99
Black Jack *62*, 64
Books, recommended 37, 52, 54,
    57, 60, 65, 84, 93, 97, 101, 120, 122
Bradbury Wilkinson 34, 47
Bremen stamps *18*
British Columbia Stamps 56
British Guiana stamps *32*
British Philatelic Association 80, 116
Britnor, Leonard E. 112
Bulgarian stamps *76, 78*

Canada
–group collecting 56 *et seq*
–stamps *21, 56–59, 77*
Canadian Philatelic Society of
    Great Britain 57
Cancels 97 *et seq*
–Maltese cross 20
Cards 88 *et seq, 89, 91, 92, 95*, 97,
    98, 121
Catalogues 21, 24, 120, *121*
Cavallini 12, 16
Christmas stamps 47, *48, 54, 56, 75*
Chalmers, James 16, 18
Christmas card, first ever *106*
Cinderella Stamp Club 80
Cinderellas 80 *et seq*
Clay tablet *8*
Clubs 80
Cole, Sir Henry 104
Collecting methods 40 *et seq*
Collectors Club 123
Colony of Canada stamps 56
Commonwealth stamps 50, 51, 52
Control letter and number *43, 47*
Corbould, Henry 30
Couriers, early *8*, 9
Courvoisier 35
Covers (*see also* First Day Covers)
    24, *54, 58, 62, 64, 66*, 88 *et seq,*
    93, 94, 98, 106, 107, 111, 122
Crawford Library 122
Cuba stamps *79*
Cuneiform script *8*

Cursores 9
Cylinder numbers *31, 47*

De la Rue 24, 31, 36, 68
Dease, Rosalind *48*, 51
Delrieu 35
Departmentals 53
Dockwra marks *13*, 99
Dockwra Penny Post Pamphlet *11*
Dockwra, William 11, 99
Dodge, J. W. 64
Dominica stamps *73*
Dulac, Edmund 33

East Anglia Postal History Study
    Circle 113
East German stamp *78*
East India Comapny 21
Engraving *28, 29*
Envelopes *18, 50*, 88, *89, 98, 101,*
    111
Essex Postal History Group 113
Exhibiting 74, 116 *et seq, 118, 119*
–advice on thematic displays 74–76
–annotation 74
–rules 76
Exhibitions 120, *123*

Fakes 80
Falkland Islands stamps *32*
Fiji stamps *35*
First Day Covers *52, 58, 75*, 88 *et*
    seq, 91, 92, 93
–albums 93
Fiscals 80
Forces Postal History 113
Fores envelopes 88, *111*
Forgeries 80
Forster, R. K. 101
Free franks *13, 105*, 108 *et seq*
Frere, Sir Bartle 21
Fujeira stamp *78*

Gabor, Eva *117*
General Post Office, formation 12
Ghana stamps *35*
Gibbons, Stanley 21, 96
Gibraltar stamps *35*
Great Britain
–group collecting 44 *et seq*
–stamps 24, *26, 30, 31, 43–53, 81,*
    85, 92, 94, 95, 113
Great Exhibition, 1851 *31*
Greece stamp *78*
Guinea stamps *75*
Gum 32, 48, 120

Hammet, Sir Benjamin 108
Hanover stamp *21*
Harrison and Sons Ltd 33, 35, 47
Hawaii stamp *30*
Hendy, John 100
Hill, Rowland 16, *17*, 88, 104
Holland stamps 77
Horowicz, Kay 76
Hungary stamps *73, 75, 78, 95, 117*

India stamps *10*
International Reply Coupon *83*
Iraq stamps *35*

Jackson, Andrew 64
Japan stamp *78*
Jugoslavia stamp *79*

Labels *81*
Lady McLeod private issue *18*, 20
Latvian stamps *27*
Legrand, Dr 30, 32
Letter cards 96
Letter sorting
–hand *17*
–electronic 26
Libraries 122
Lincoln, William 97
Link House Publications 80
Literature 120
Locals 16, *36*, 80
London Postal History Group 113
Luton and District Philatelic Society
    80
Luxembourg stamp 76

Macao stamp *35*
Machin, Arnold 47, 48
Machin definitives 47 *et seq, 48*
Magazines 21, *123*
Mail coaches *2, 6, 22, 38, 70, 86,*
    102, 114
–guard *15*
–guns *107*
–tokens *107*
Mail trains
–guard *42*
–US fast mail *63*
Malagasy stamp *35*
Malawi stamp *35*
Maltese cross cancellation *20*, 100
Maritime mail 110
Mauritius stamps *90*
Maury, Arthur 21
Millar, Rev Ernest 31
Moens, J. B. 21
Montserrat stamp *78*
Morris, Robert H. 62
Mullick, Beman *41*
Mulready, William 16, 88
Mulready
–envelopes 88, *90*, 96
–wrappers 16

Naphthadag 25, 26
National Philatelic Society 123
National Postal Museum 122
Netherlands stamps *27*
New Brunswick stamps *21*, 56, *58*
New South Wales stamps 53
New Zealand
–group collecting 60
–stamps *60–61, 91*
Newfoundland stamps 56, *56*
Nova Scotia stamps *21*, 56

Odontometre 30
Overprints 72

Paper, for stamp production 24, 26
Papua and New Guinea stamp *76*
Penny Black 16, *20, 24, 43,* 44, *44,*
   45, 92
Penny Red *43,* 46
Perforations 30
Perkins Bacon 33
—printing machine *24*
Phantoms 80
Phosphor bands 26
Pillar box designs *109*
Polish Postal History Society of
   Great Britain 113
Polyvinyl alcohol gum 48
Post cards 96
Post Office illustrations
—in 1790 *12*
—St Martins-le-Grand *13*
Post Office Records Office 112
Postage rates 12
Postal administrations 21
Postal history 8 *et seq,* 104 *et seq*
—research 112
—societies 113
Postal History Society 113
Postal services
—early 8 *et seq*
—first national 10
—first public 10
—government monopoly 12
—Thurn and Taxis 10
—US Carriers 16
Postal stationery 16, 93 *et seq*
Postal wagons 10
Postmarks (*see also* Bishop marks)
12, *98,* 99, *99, 101, 116*
Postmen
—country letter carrier, 1842 *14*
—uniforms *17*
Pre-cancels *67*
Prince Edward Island stamps 56
Printing errors *36, 46,* 48
—on Machin definitives 48
Printing methods 33 *et seq*
—colloidal graphite *25*
—colour separation *34*
—die-stamping 37
—embossing *33,* 37
—engraving *28, 29*
—lithography *35,* 36
—photography *36,* 37
—photogravure *35,* 36
—recess 33
—typography 36
Propaganda labels 80
Provisionals 62, 64, *66*
Prussia stamp *21*

Queen Elizabeth II stamps 50, 51
   56
Queensland stamps 53
Quester, Matthew de 12
Quetta earthquake cover 104, *107*

Registration labels 80, 84
Regumming 33

Robertson, Alan W. 110
Roulettes 32
Royal Philatelic Society 123

Sample stamps *37*
Scott, J. W. 21
Scott Publishing Company 96
Sharjah stamp *78*
Societies 116
Society of Postal Historians 113
South Australia stamps 53
Southern Rhodesia stamp *36*
Spain stamps *21, 79*
Stamp booklets 49, *50*
Stamps
—condition of 118
—early *21*
—first adhesive 16
—first perforated *24*
—production 24 *et seq*
—rare *21*
—samples 37
—self adhesive 51
—unaccepted designs *112*
Stanhope, Lord 12
Stonehouse, John *41*
Strike posts 84
Sudanese stamps *112*
Sweden stamp *77*
Switzerland stamps *21, 32, 77*

Tasmania stamps 53
Telegraph 80, *81*
Tête-bêche stamps *32, 47*
Thematic collecting (*see also*
Themes) 72 *et seq*
—clubs 80
—exhibitions 80
—sources of supply 76
Themes
—archaeology *78*
—artists and paintings *79*
—astronomy *119*
—birds *73*
—butterflies and moths *61, 76*
—Christmas *47, 48, 54, 56, 75*
—fairy tales *76, 117*
—flowers *73*
—printing and press *72–74, 77*
—railways *76*
—sailors *77*
—war 72
Thurn and Taxis posts 10
Topics, *see* Themes
Tuke, Sir Brian 10
Tuscany stamp *21*
Twopenny Blue 44

Uganda stamp *31*
Uniform Penny Post 16, 88
United Nations stamps *28, 65*
United States of America
—group collecting 62 *et seq*
—stamps *62–69, 75*
Universal Postal Union 20
Upper Volta stamp *78*
Upper Yafa, South Arabia stamps
   78, 79

Van Diemens Land stamps 53
Velayer, Rupert de 16
Veredarii 9
Victoria stamps 53
Victorian stamp box 104

Wallace, Robert 16
Waterlow and Sons 37
Watermark detectors 30
Watermarks 26
Waterton Collection *81*
Wells Fargo stamps *108*
West German stamps *76,* 77
Western Australia stamps 53, *54*
Witherings, Thomas 12
Wrappers 16, 96
Wurtemberg stamp *21*
Wyon, William 30, 33

Zemstvo stamps *82, 83*
Zenkov stamp *82*
Zolotonosha stamp *82*
Zurich stamps 20, *35*

Acknowledgments

Pictures numbered 42, 74, 344 are of items in the Royal Philatelic Collection, and are reproduced by gracious permission of Her Majesty The Queen. Other acknowledgments are due as follows:

Acheson Colloids Ltd 43—47
Bradbury Wilkinson and Co Ltd 76
British Army Public Relations Service 364
Campbell's Press Studios Ltd 401
Bruce Castle 387·
City Museum and Art Gallery, Birmingham 409
De La Rue Collection 68, 256, 398
French Postal Museum 4
Stanley Gibbons Ltd. 40
Great Britain Philatelic Society 30
Guildhall Library 17, 94
H. R. Harmer Ltd 31, 71, 72, 227, 228, 257, 357, 361
Library of Congress, Washington 225
Link House 41, 140, 325, 345, 408, 411—413, 418
London Stamp Exchange 224, 243, 383, 393
Mansell Collection 1, 104, 392
Museum of Postal History, The Hague 94
National Postal Museum 25, 63, 96, 98
Post Office 8, 9, 16, 18, 28, 75, 110—113, 134, 136—139, 338, 391, 395, 396, 397
    (The Post Office also supplied the seven mail coach pictures used at the beginning of each chapter)
Proud-Bailey Co Ltd 373
Robson Lowe Ltd 73, 86, 90, 91, 105
Gerald Sattin Collection 27
United Nations 58—62, 229—241
Victoria and Albert Museum 384